VISUAL QUICKSTART GUIDE

BBEDIT 4

FOR MACINTOSH

Mark R. Bell

Peachpit Press

Visual QuickStart Guide
BBEdit 4 for Macintosh
Mark R. Bell

Peachpit Press
1249 Eighth Street
Berkeley, CA 94710
(800) 283-9444
(510) 524-2178
(510) 524-2221 (fax)

Find us on the World Wide Web at: http://www.peachpit.com

Peachpit Press is a division of Addison Wesley Longman

Editor: Marjorie Baer
Copy editor: Virginia Smith
Indexer: Emily Glossbrenner
Production: David Van Ness
Inhouse production: Amy Changar
Cover design: The Visual Group

Notice of rights

Notice of liability

ISBN: 0-201-69659-2

0 9 8 7 6 5 4 3 2 1

Printed and bound in the United States of America

Printed on recycled paper

Dedication:

To Bailey, for her relentless entertainment skills, and of course, Virginia, for surviving our first year of marriage with style and grace despite hurricanes, houses, books, jobs, and, oh yeah, the Morley.

Thanks to:

Sandra Schneible, an asset to Bare Bones, for putting me in touch with Peachpit and helping along the way.

Nolan Hester, for sticking it out through the longest proposal in recorded history.

Marjorie Baer, editor supreme, for an unbelievable amount of patience, fortitude throughout the whole process, and for making every suggestion a good one.

Virginia Smith, my copy-editing wife, for keeping me from making a fool of myself with the English language.

Amy Changar, for her production skills.

Emily Glossenbrenner, for accepting the job of indexing this book on about five minutes notice.

David Van Ness, for laying out this book on a schedule so tight, you'd think he didn't have anything else to do but wait on me.

Tristan Reid, for his help with scripting.

Debbie Suggs, for her work on the appendices—yet another job well done.

Gregg and Mary Catherine, for waiting. And waiting. And waiting...

TABLE OF CONTENTS

TABLE OF CONTENTS

Introduction

Welcome to BBEdit! If BBEdit is new to you, then you're in for a real treat. With this Visual Quickstart Guide, you'll be able to use BBEdit to easily create Hypertext Markup Language (HTML) documents that incorporate all the styles and features used by the latest versions of Netscape Navigator and Internet Explorer, including:

- multiple headings
- background images
- styled and colored text
- frames
- style sheets
- horizontal rules
- lists
- tables
- forms
- images

Experienced BBEdit users will also be able to write and edit computer code and send PowerTalk mail, as well as manage large Web sites through BBEdit's powerful search-and-replace and scripting capabilities.

One of the coolest—but least known—facts about BBEdit is that it is extensible, which means that programmers of commercial and shareware software can write plug-ins for BBEdit that extend its capabilities even further. Thanks to this type of flexibility, new uses for BBEdit are popping up all the time.

What Is BBEdit?

What exactly is BBEdit? For starters, BBEdit is the premier text editor for the Macintosh operating system. That's not how it got started or how most people use it today, however. In the beginning, BBEdit was a tool employed by computer programmers to write software code for applications like Adobe Photoshop and ClarisWorks. Along the way, people realized that BBEdit worked very well for editing HTML documents for use on the World Wide Web.

Since HTML documents, like computer code, consist of ASCII text, programmers naturally deduced that if they could write computer code with BBEdit, they could use it for writing HTML as well. As the interest in creating HTML documents moved beyond computer programmers to people like you and me, BBEdit became a smash hit with everyday HTML authors. BBEdit is so popular, in fact, that it is the tool of choice on the majority of Web sites that are managed with the Mac OS—and that's something like 67 percent of all Web sites!

Figure 1.1 BBEdit is a the most powerful text and HTML editor available for the Mac OS.

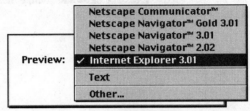

Figure 1.2 You can customize BBEdit to work with any Web browser.

Figure 1.3 You can preview your work using the only graphical interface that counts—a Web browser.

Figure 1.4 BBEdit's HTML Tools palette can be customized to show only the items you use on a regular basis. Also, it is extensible through plug-ins, similar to the way that Web browsers view additional kinds of data through plug-ins.

Figure 1.5 You can create groups of commonly used files or associated files for easy access.

Figure 1.6 Disk browsers offer easy access to your hard drives and help you locate certain types of files, such as HTML documents, images, and project groups.

Why Use BBEdit?

What makes BBEdit so popular? In my opinion, it boils down to this: Even the most sophisticated graphical HTML editor doesn't let you exercise absolute control over the HTML code generated by the program. BBEdit, on the other hand, allows you to create, edit, and maintain large collections of HTML documents easily, and with the precision of a surgeon.

HTML is constantly being restandardized by international organizations like the Institute of Electrical and Electronics Engineers (IEEE), International Organization for Standardization (ISO), American National Standards Institute (ANSI), and the World Wide Web Consortium (W3C). Because these organizations are so slow to approve changes, companies like Netscape and Microsoft simply forge ahead and implement their own changes.

Because BBEdit doesn't use a graphical interface (known in computer-speak as a WYSIWYG—what you see is what you get—editor), it doesn't lock you into a fixed set of HTML formatting capabilities the way an HTML editor with a graphical interface does. As the makers of BBEdit, Bare Bones Software, say about using a graphical HTML editor, "What You See Ain't What You Get." I've never found a graphical HTML editor that could do everything I need it to do to create my kind of HTML document. Some have come close, but I've always turned to BBEdit when I needed to fix errors in the code, add additional code, or make changes to multiple documents simultaneously.

Text As Data

HTML is nothing more than plain ASCII text arranged in such a way that Web browsers interpret and display it according to a pre-defined set of rules. So an HTML document starts out as text and results in something much more when viewed through a Web browser—complex multimedia data.

HTML is what is known as a markup language (that's what the ML stands for in HTML), rather than a programming language per se. It is a subset (the hypertext subset, hence HT) of the Standardized General Markup Language, or SGML. This type of data is can be arranged with great flexibility and variety and still be properly interpreted by a Web browser. That's what makes authoring HTML documents at once easy and challenging.

BBEdit helps you arrange your data within an HTML document so that it's easy for you to read, search, and replace. Its ability to manip-ulate huge amounts of data in a single file or in multiple documents makes it perhaps the most powerful text editor for any platform—Mac OS, Windows NT, Unix. You can find and replace a single word in a single document, or you can perform a pattern search and replace in documents in multiple folders.

Figure 1.7 BBEdit works with several types of textual data, including ASCII text files, HTML files, and Perl scripts (shown here).

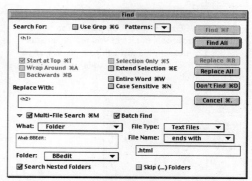

Figure 1.8 Using BBEdit, data can be manipulated in many ways, one of the most important of which is making complex changes using its superior find and replace capabilities.

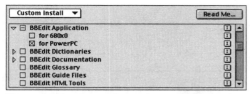

Figure 1.9 You can install one of several versions of BBEdit, depending on the type of processor in your computer.

Figure 1.10 The commercial version of BBEdit, which is covered in this book, has many options not found in the Lite version.

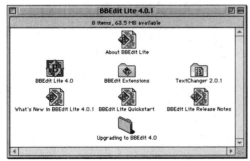

Figure 1.11 BBEdit Lite is nonetheless a great solution for editing text files and HTML documents. It's free, but not nearly as flexible as the commercial version.

Hardware & Software Requirements

BBEdit has very modest hardware and software requirements. It will run on any Macintosh based on the Motorola 68K processor and any Macintosh or Macintosh clone with a PowerPC processor. You must be running System 7 or higher.

If you have a PowerPC-based computer, you can install either the PowerPC-native version of BBEdit or a FAT binary, which will run on either the PowerPC or the 68K. Non-PowerPC users may install the 68K or fat binary versions. If you're not sure what type of computer you have or the version of the operating system, the installation program's Easy Install option will determine this for you and install the version that is most appropriate for your computer. **Figure 1.9** shows some of the choices you'll have when installing BBEdit for these two types of processors.

Installing BBEdit

There are two versions of BBEdit, a commercial version that comes on a CD-ROM and costs about $100 (see **Figure 1.10**), and a freeware version called BBEdit Lite that you can download from dozens of locations on the Web (see **Figure 1.11**). The current commercial version is 4.5.1, and the freeware version is 4.0.1. The Lite version doesn't contain all the features of the commercial version, and although the demo version is just as functional as the commercial version, it doesn't let you save any of your work. This book is intended for users of the commercial version.

REQUIREMENTS / INSTALLING BBEDIT

Obtaining BBEdit

You can download a demo version of BBEdit and a fully functional copy of BBEdit Lite from the Bare Bones Web site at the following URL, shown in **Figure 1.12**:

http://www.barebones.com

Wherever possible, I'll compare features of the commercial version with those of the Lite version because there are many tens of thousands of BBEdit Lite users out there, but keep in mind that this book is intended for users of the commercial version.

Running the Installer

To install BBEdit and its associated files, insert the CD and double-click the Install BBEdit 4.5 icon (see **Figure 1.13**). You'll have several installation options, including:

- Easy Install—installs BBEdit 4.5, BBEdit Table Builder, spelling dictionaries, standard BBEdit plug-ins, HTML authoring tools, documentation, and helper applications. Requires about 21MB of disk space.

- Custom Install—allows you to select exactly what components are to be installed, which can occupy from 2MB to 30MB of disk space.

✔ Tip

- If you have the space available on your hard drive, choose the Easy Install option.

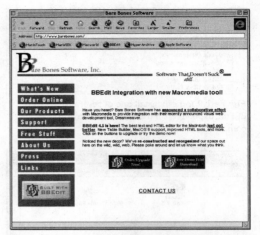

Figure 1.12 Visit the Bare Bones home page for the latest information on BBEdit as well as valuable resources on publishing HTML documents and managing Web sites.

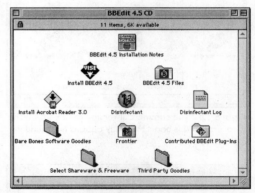

Figure 1.13 The BBEdit CD-ROM contains the BBEdit installation program as well as many other utilities and programs.

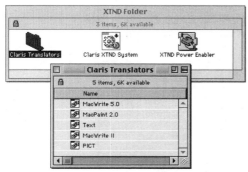

Figure 1.14 BBEdit is capable of opening, editing, and saving documents created by traditional word processors such as MacWrite and Microsoft Word, depending on which translators are installed.

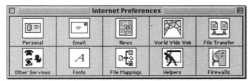

Figure 1.15 Internet Config is an application that helps programs like BBEdit work with other applications used for or with the Internet.

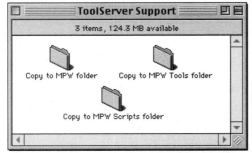

Figure 1.16 ToolServer support is needed only if you plan to work in programming environments supported by Apple's Essentials, Tools, and Objects (ETO).

Additional Software

In addition to the BBEdit application and its helper files and documentation, the installation process may also load several other pieces of software, depending on your installation choices. Some of them play an active role in how you'll use BBEdit to work with HTML documents and maintain Web sites, and so you'll learn about them later in the book. The others are intended more for programmers who will be writing software code, a task not given much attention in this book. Specifically, the additional software will allow you to perform file conversions and take advantage of other Internet services, as well as access additional programming environments. These programs are

1. Claris XTEND—a collection of system extensions that enable BBEdit to read and write documents created with certain word processing programs like ClarisWorks or Microsoft Word (see **Figure 1.14**). This is helpful when you're collaborating with people who have created HTML documents with these programs rather than BBEdit.

2. Internet Config—program that enables BBEdit to communicate with your favorite Internet applications, as well as identify BBEdit as your HTML editor of choice to other Internet Config–aware applications such as Internet Explorer, Eudora, and Fetch (see **Figure 1.15**).

3. ToolServer—a collection of BBEdit extensions that allow BBEdit to interact with many programming environments that support Apple's Essentials, Tools, and Objects (ETO) features. It's advisable to make sure the Claris XTND and Internet Config files are installed. ToolServer support is installed automatically by the Easy Install option, and it's OK to leave it on your hard drive even if you're not a programmer.

ADDITIONAL SOFTWARE

Installed Files & Folders

Depending on the installation options you choose, BBEdit will install hundreds of folders and files on your hard drive. The majority of these will be located in the BBEdit folder itself, including the BBEdit and BBEdit Table Builder applications and Apple Guide documents. In addition to these files, the following folders will be installed:

1. BBEdit Plug-Ins—files that add features to BBEdit, such as the ability to open, edit, and save HTML documents via FTP (see **Figure 1.17**).

2. BBEdit Glossary—documents whose contents may be inserted into other documents with a keystroke or button click (see **Figure 1.18**).

3. BBEdit Dictionaries—dictionaries used by BBEdit's spelling checker, including dictionaries for most major languages as well as a custom dictionary (see **Figure 1.19**).

Figure 1.17 BBEdit uses plug-ins to extend its text-manipulation capabilities, as well as add networking features like FTP.

Figure 1.18 Create glossary entries to store commonly used tags and data.

Figure 1.19 BBEdit can use multiple dictionaries in conjunction with its built-in spelling checker.

Figure 1.20 BBEdit is scriptable, and you can add frequently used scripts to its Scripts menu.

Figure 1.21 Place documents in the BBEdit Startup Items folder to have them automatically launched by BBEdit.

Figure 1.22 You can use templates with BBEdit to save time when creating new documents to ensure that similar documents maintain a consistent style

Figure 1.23 BBEdit creates several Preferences files, some of which can be automatically backed up in case the original should be corrupted or accidentally erased.

4. BBEdit Scripts—AppleScripts that you may add, modify, or delete, and that work in conjunction with BBEdit to perform routine tasks (see **Figure 1.20**).

5. BBEdit Startup Items—documents (or aliases to documents) that will automatically open when BBEdit is launched (see **Figure 1.21**).

6. HTML Templates—documents that contain commands for BBEdit to perform, such as insert a predefined header or footer (see **Figure 1.22**).

7. Preferences (System Folder)—several different Preferences files are stored here, including a new BBEdit Grep Patterns file, which allows you to preserve your grep patterns even if your general preference file is thrown away (see **Figure 1.23**).

INSTALLED FILES & FOLDERS

Optimizing BBEdit

Considering how powerfully BBEdit can manipulate massive files, it uses surprisingly little memory. As with most applications for the Mac OS, you can tell BBEdit to use more or less memory if necessary. BBEdit requires about 2MB of memory if Virtual Memory is turned off in the Memory Control Panel or if you don't have a memory-enhancement tool such as Ram Doubler installed. In **Figure 1.24**, I have more than doubled BBEdit's memory allocation because I want to open several dozen files simultaneously.

You can allocate as little as 700K of memory to BBEdit with virtual memory turned on, or as much as your computer has free to allocate to applications. Try starting off with the recommended amount (1000K with virtual memory on) and give it more if necessary. Of course, you'll know when this is the case when you get an error message like "BBEdit cannot perform this function because not enough memory is available." A good rule of thumb is to start off by doubling the amount of memory for an application, then cut back as long as the error doesn't reappear.

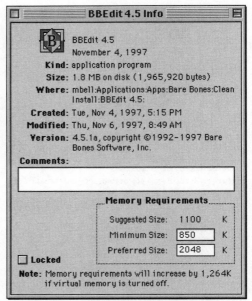

Figure 1.24 You can adjust the amount of memory BBEdit uses by selecting the BBEdit application icon and choosing Command+I or Get Info from the File menu in the Finder.

Editing Text

BBEdit lets you to edit text using all the methods pioneered by the Mac OS: pointing, clicking, highlighting, copying, cutting, and pasting—concepts that should be familiar to anyone who's ever used a Mac. BBEdit, however, adds an entirely new dimension to editing text through dozens of features not found in most text editors such as TeachText or SimpleText. It's these high-octane text-editing features that make BBEdit so powerful.

In this chapter, we'll look at BBEdit's most important text-editing features. Some of these features may be a bit intimidating at first, especially if you're unfamiliar with BBEdit. Others will seem more natural, and you'll probably think to yourself, "Oh, that works a lot like my word processor."

If some features seem strange or awkward at first, remember: BBEdit got its start as a programming tool. To be a successful programmer, you sometimes have to do things the hard way—if you make it look too easy, then other programmers will think you're just not working hard enough!

Once you've mastered the basics of editing text and spent more time using BBEdit's advanced features, they will become second nature. Then when you use your favorite word processor, you'll find yourself saying, "I wish this worked the same way as BBEdit!"

Creating & Saving New Documents

BBEdit works like most applications when it comes to creating and saving new documents, in that you can use the File pull-down menu (see **Figure 2.1**) or a keyboard combination to create and save documents.

To create a new file:

- Choose File | New and select from the following options:–

  –Text Document (or Command+N)

  –Text Document with selection (or Shift+Command+N)

  –Text Document with clipboard (or Shift+Option+Command+N)

  –HTML Document (or Control+Command+N)

Selecting a new text document will open a blank document like the one shown in **Figure 2.2**, while selecting a new HTML document will open a dialog box containing several default settings associated with an HTML document, as in **Figure 2.3**.

✔ Tip

- There are a few other options under the File | New menu. We'll take a look at these in Appendix A, "Menu Items."

After you have typed one or more characters (even a blank space), you will be able to save the new document. A small black diamond in the upper left-hand corner indicates that changes have been made and the Save option is now active, as in **Figure 2.4**.

To save a document, choose File | Save (or Command+S) and give the document a name, as in **Figure 2.5**. We'll talk more about additional options associated with saving documents later.

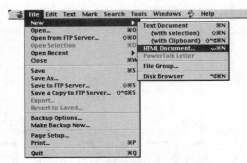

Figure 2.1 A new feature of BBEdit 4.5.1 is the File | New menu, where you'll go to create all your new documents.

Figure 2.2 Creating a new text document.

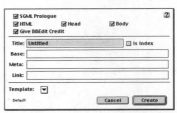

Figure 2.3 BBEdit simplifies creating a new HTML document by providing a single place to enter several important pieces of information.

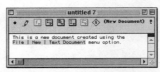

Figure 2.4 BBEdit offers visual clues to indicate whether or not a document needs to be saved, including the black diamond in the status bar.

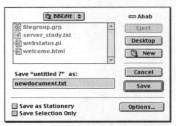

Figure 2.5 The standard Save As dialog box.

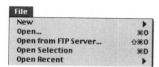

Figure 2.6 The File menu offers several ways to open an existing document.

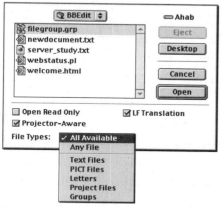

Figure 2.7 BBEdit can open several types of documents, including text and HTML files.

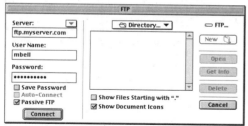

Figure 2.8 Documents may be opened from and saved to FTP servers, which is especially useful when working with Web servers running under operating systems other than the Mac OS.

Figure 2.9 Use the Open Selection option as a shortcut when working with several related files that are referenced in one another, as in this example.

Opening Existing Documents

You can use BBEdit to open any ASCII text file, HTML document, or PICT image. You may open them one at a time through the File menu, a portion of which is shown in **Figure 2.6**; or you may select multiple documents in the Finder and open them simultaneously by dragging and dropping them onto the BBEdit application icon, or by selecting File | Open (or Command+O). If you select a text document whose file type creator is not BBEdit and double-click on it (or choose Command+O), it will not be opened by BBEdit.

To open an existing document:

- Choose File | Open (or Command+O) and locate a document using the standard dialog box presented (see **Figure 2.7**).

- Choose File | Open from FTP Server (or Shift+Command+O) to open a document from an FTP server (see **Figure 2.8**).

- To open a document whose name appears within another BBEdit document, highlight the document name and select File | Open Selection (or Command+D). BBEdit will look for this document in the same folder in which the first document is located; if it doesn't find it, you'll be prompted to locate the document. For example, **Figure 2.9** shows a document called welcome.html highlighted within a document called newdocument.txt, which has just been opened using Open Selection.

- Choose File | Open Recent to see a chrono-logical list of up to 10 documents recently open by BBEdit, as in **Figure 2.10**.

- To open several documents simultaneously through the BBEdit application, hold down the Option key while selecting File | Open (or Command+O) to reveal the Open Several option, shown in **Figure 2.11**.

✔ Tip

- You can also open files from an FTP server. We'll cover this in Chapter 5, "HTML Tools."

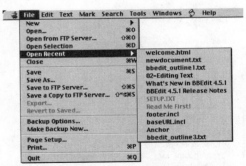

Figure 2.10 BBEdit tracks your 10 most recently accessed documents and provides a shortcut to them through the Open Recent option in the File menu.

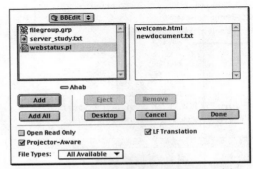

Figure 2.11 A unique feature with BBEdit is its ability to open multiple documents through the File menu.

OPENING EXISTING DOCUMENTS

Figure 2.12 Use the mouse to drag and highlight a portion of text.

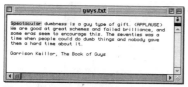

Figure 2.13 Double-click on a word to highlight it.

Figure 2.14 To highlight an entire line of text, triple-click anywhere on that line.

Figure 2.15 Hold down the Command key while triple-clicking to highlight an entire paragraph.

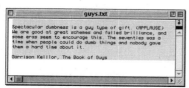

Figure 2.16 Use good-old Command+A to select all the text in a document.

Basic Editing

Now that you know how to create, save, and open text documents, let's look at some of the basic editing options available in BBEdit. First, let's consider the ways in which you can select text. Then we'll quickly discuss the ways you can move and drag and drop text, as well as how to move around within a document.

✔ Tip

- BBEdit allows you to perform multiple undos by selecting Edit | Undo (or Command+Z). The number of undos will be limited by the amount of memory available to BBEdit and the size of the working document.

Selecting text:

1. To highlight a text string of any length, position the cursor at the location where you want to begin your selection. Point and click the cursor by holding down the mouse button, then drag the cursor to the end point of your selection and release the mouse button (see **Figure 2.12**).

2. To highlight a single word, double-click on that word, as in **Figure 2.13**.

3. To select an entire line, triple-click anywhere on that line or choose Edit | Select Line (or press Command+L), as in **Figure 2.14.**

4. To highlight an entire paragraph, triple-click on that paragraph while holding down the Command key, as in **Figure 2.15.**

5. To highlight the contents of an entire document, choose Edit | Select All (or press Command+A), as in **Figure 2.16.**

6. To highlight the contents of the line to the right of the insertion point, place the cursor where you want your selection to begin and press Shift+Command+Right Arrow, as in **Figure 2.17**.

7. To highlight the contents of the line to the left of the insertion point, place the cursor where you want your selection to begin and press Shift+Command+Left Arrow, as in **Figure 2.18**.

8. To highlight the contents of the entire document up to the insertion point, place the cursor where you want your selection to begin and press Shift+Command+Up Arrow, as in **Figure 2.19**.

9. To highlight the contents of the entire document from the insertion point forward, place the cursor where you want your selection to begin and press Shift+Command+Down Arrow, as in **Figure 2.20**.

Moving text:

1. To copy text for insertion into another location or document, highlight the text and select Edit | Copy, or Command+C, or F3.

2. To delete text or remove it from one location and place it in another, highlight the text and select Edit | Cut, or Command+X, or F2.

3. To insert text that has been copied or cut from another location, insert the cursor at the target location and select Edit | Paste, or Command+V, or F4.

4. To forward delete one character at a time, press the Del key.

5. To forward delete one word at a time, press Option+Del.

6. To forward delete to the end of a line, press Command+Option+Del.

Figure 2.17 Use Shift+Command+Right Arrow to highlight text to the right of the cursor.

Figure 2.18 Use Shift+Command+Left Arrow to highlight text to the left of the cursor.

Figure 2.19 Use Shift+Command+Up Arrow to highlight text above and to the left of the cursor.

Figure 2.20 Use Shift+Command+Down Arrow to highlight text below and to the right of the cursor.

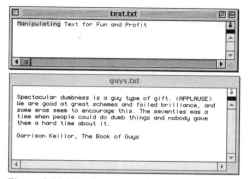

Figure 2.21 Select the text you want to move to another location within the same document, or to another BBEdit document, as in this example.

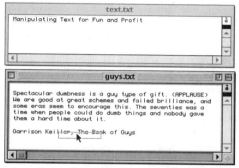

Figure 2.22 BBEdit fully supports drag and drop, which makes moving text easier than cutting and pasting.

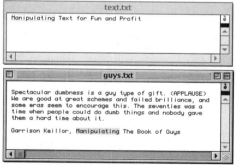

Figure 2.23 The example document after dragging and dropping the text from one document into another.

Dragging and dropping text:

To move or copy a chunk of text from one location in a document to another, or from one BBEdit document to another:

1. Highlight the text to be moved or copied, as in **Figure 2.21**.

2. Drag (see **Figure 2.22**) and drop (see **Figure 2.23**) the text into the new location.

Moving around in a document:

1. To move to the very beginning of a document, press Command+Up Arrow.

2. To move to the very end of a document, press Command+Down Arrow.

3. To move to the end of a line, press Command+Right Arrow.

4. To move to the beginning of a line, press Command+Left Arrow.

5. To scroll up, press Page Up.

6. To scroll down, press Page Down.

Keypad Shortcuts

You may also use the numbers on the numeric keypad to navigate the cursor in a document once you have selected the Keypad Cursor Controls option from the Edit | Preferences | Editor dialog window. The numbers and their equivalent controls are:

1 End of Line	**5** Show Selection
2 Down	**6** Right
3 Scroll Down	**7** Start of Line
4 Left	**8** Up
	9 Scroll Up

BASIC EDITING

Using Windows

Each BBEdit document window provides easy access to information about the document, as well as special features that make editing text as easy as possible. These features help set BBEdit apart from all other text editors and allow you to customize your own editing environment.

The status bar:

The status bar may be hidden or shown, as in **Figure 2.24**, and provides easy access to:

1. Information about whether the document has changed. A solid diamond indicates that the contents of the document have changed; a hollow diamond indicates the window location has changed, but the content has not (see **Figure 2.25**).

2. The Pencil icon, shown in **Figure 2.26**, allows you to write-protect a document or remove write protection, whereas the diagonal slash says that write protection is already on.

3. The Function pop-up menu, shown in **Figure 2.27**, provides access to programming functions (if installed).

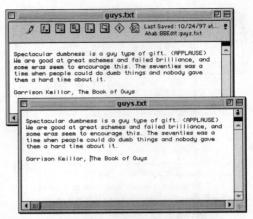

Figure 2.24 The status bar provides easy access to additional information, but isn't necessary to view a document.

Figure 2.25 The hollow or solid diamonds indicate if a window's position or content has changed.

Figure 2.26 To easily write-protect or unprotect a document, just click the Pencil icon in the status bar.

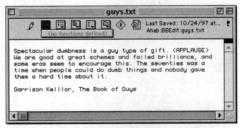

Figure 2.27 The Function pop-up menu provides access to defined functions.

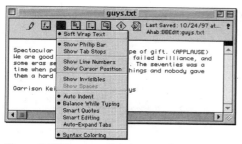

Figure 2.28 The status bar also provides access to the Window Options menu.

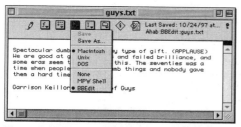

Figure 2.29 The File menu is loaded with options to change the way BBEdit displays documents.

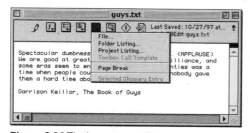

Figure 2.30 The Insert menu allows you to insert data into a document.

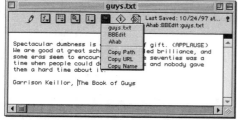

Figure 2.31 Select the Path menu in the status bar to reveal a document's path.

4. The Window Options menu, shown in **Figure 2.28**, allows you to change many attributes of a window, including wrapping text and showing line numbers and cursor position.

5. The File menu, shown in **Figure 2.29**, lets you save the document and change line-break options (Macintosh, Unix, or DOS).

6. The Insert menu, shown in **Figure 2.30**, provides easy access to files and information that may be inserted into a document.

7. The Path menu, shown in **Figure 2.31**, reveals the path to the working document.

8. The Info button displays information about the document, as in the example shown in **Figure 2.32**.

9. The Document icon, when clicked, reveals the location of the working document in the Finder.

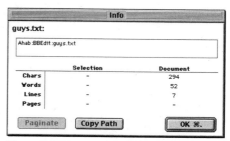

Figure 2.32 To get more information about a document, select the Info icon in the status bar.

USING WINDOWS

The split bar:

The split bar allows you to divide a window into two autonomously scrolling regions, as in **Figure 2.33**. This is useful when you need to access a portion of a long document and don't want to scroll up and down every time you want to refer to it. To use the split bar:

1. Grab the split bar handle with the cursor and drag it down.

2. Scroll to the desired sections in each window.

3. To remove the split bar, drag the handle back up to the top of the document.

Figure 2.33 Use the split bar to divide a document into two regions.

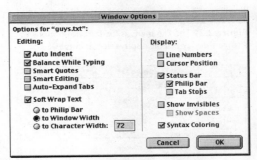

Figure 2.34 The Window Options menu allows you to customize a specific window and override the global window options.

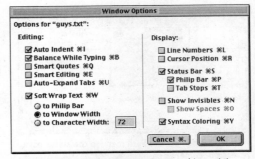

Figure 2.35 Holding down the Command key while selecting the Window Options menu reveals its keyboard shortcuts.

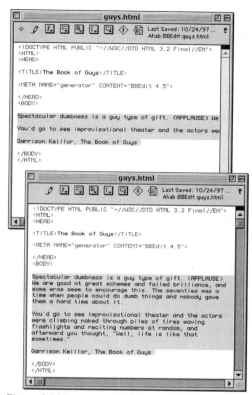

Figure 2.36 Two views of the same document: unwrapped text (above) and wrapped text (below).

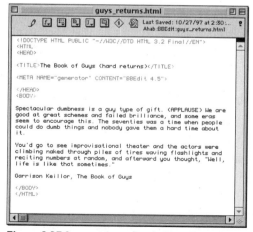

Figure 2.37 Syntax color coding helps make editing an HTML document easier than if all the text were black.

Changing window options:

Each window is configurable through the Edit | Window Options menu (or by pressing Command+Option+;), shown in **Figure 2.34**. Many of the configuration options here are self-explanatory; each of them is covered in Appendices A and B. To reveal the keyboard shortcuts for the window options, hold down the Command key while selecting Edit | Window Options (see **Figure 2.35**).

As an HTML author, the features that you're most likely to be concerned with here are the following:

1. Soft Wrap Text—allows lines longer than the width of your screen to be wrapped to the next line. **Figure 2.36** shows how three long lines of text can be displayed more efficiently when wrapped. See the following section for more information about how BBEdit wraps different kinds of text.

2. Status Bar—provides easy access to shortcuts and features (see above).

3. Syntax Coloring—displays certain HTML and programming commands in predefined colors, as in **Figure 2.37**. This enables you to more easily read HTML code.

Wrapping Text

BBEdit is very flexible when it comes to wrapping text, which is a good thing for HTML authors because of the different ways in which Web browsers and text editors for the Mac OS, DOS, and Unix handle wrapped text. This is especially important for those of us who maintain Web sites that reside on non-Mac OS Web servers, such as Windows NT and Unix servers.

We've seen how BBEdit can wrap or unwrap text in a window (see **Figure 2.36**), but this is only part of the issue. BBEdit wraps text in two ways:

1. Soft wrap—text is wrapped to the width of the window, the Philip bar, or to a predefined number of character spaces, depending on your Window Options or Preferences settings.

2. Hard wrap—text is not wrapped until you enter a hard return.

Because HTML doesn't recognize hard-wrapped text by default, any hard returns in your BBEdit documents will appear as wrapped text when viewed in a Web browser. **Figure 2.37** shows an example of multiple hard returns in an HTML document that do not appear when viewed in a Web browser (see **Figure 2.38**)

Nonetheless, using hard returns in HTML documents makes the HTML code easier to read. In fact, I don't think I've ever seen an HTML document that didn't employ hard returns.

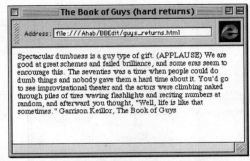

Figure 2.38 Web browsers don't recognize hard returns unless the text is "preformatted."

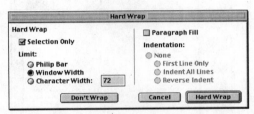

Figure 2.39 Choose HardWrap from the Text menu to change how BBEdit wraps text in a document.

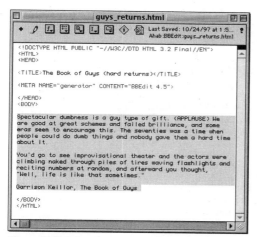

Figure 2.40 Select the text you want to convert into hard-wrapped text.

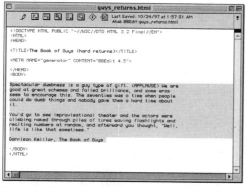

Figure 2.41 The document after converting to hard returns.

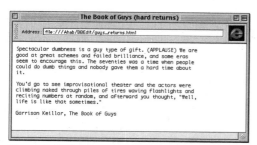

Figure 2.42 The document with preformatted text attributes applied and viewed in a Web browser.

Converting Wrapped Text

You can tell BBEdit to convert wrapped text into non-wrapped text by changing soft returns into hard returns as they appear in your window. This can be very useful when writing HTML documents that employ pre-formatted text. To replace soft returns with hard returns:

1. Choose Text | Hard Wrap (or Command+\), as in **Figure 2.39**.

2. Decide where you want the hard returns entered (Philip Bar, Window Width, or Character Width).

3. Press the Return key (or click the Hard Wrap button).

Figure 2.40 shows a sample document with soft-wrapped text, and **Figure 2.41** shows the document after hard wrapping at the Window width. The window has been widened to show exactly where the text was hard wrapped.

Finally, take a look at **Figure 2.42** to see how this document will appear in a Web browser once the preformatted text tags have been applied.

Understanding Line Breaks

BBEdit is capable of saving a document using one of three different types of line breaks. This is important if you are editing documents that reside on other types of file or Web servers.

BBEdit uses the following types of soft line breaks:

1. Macintosh—for use on any Mac OS system or one that supports Apple's Hierarchical File System (HFS) or HFS+. The ASCII equivalent is 13, and the escape character is represented as \r.

2. Unix—for use on most any Unix-based file systems, including Solaris and SunOS, and perhaps even Apple's forthcoming operating system (code-named Rhapsody). The ASCII equivalent is 10, and the escape character is represented as \n.

3. DOS—for use on any system that uses an MS-DOS-style file system, such as Windows 95 or NT. The ASCII equivalent is 10 and 13, and the escape character is represented as \r or \n.

To change a document's line breaks:

1. Choose File | Save or Save As.

2. Click the Options button in the Save dialog box.

3. Select from one of the three options, as shown in **Figure 2.43**.

✔ Tip

■ Using the incorrect type of line break could result in your HTML documents not being displayed properly.

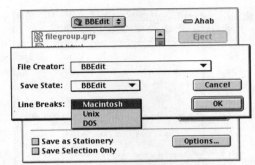

Figure 2.43 BBEdit supports multiple types of line breaks to insure compatibility between your documents and the most popular types of servers on which they may reside.

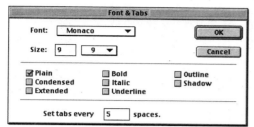

Figure 2.44 Choose Fonts & Tabs from the Text menu to change the attributes of a particular document (independently of the global settings).

Manipulating Text

BBEdit allows you to manipulate text in several ways so that you can create better HTML and programming documents. Most of the options were originally intended for programmers, but as you've probably guessed by now, these features are handy for HTML authors as well.

Changing fonts and tabs:

When working with HTML documents, using a monospaced font is a good idea—it's easier on the eye and allows you to line your text up properly when using certain tags, such as pre-formatted text. Tab stops are not as important as the proper font selection, and you can set them to as many spaces as you like.

To change fonts and tabs:

1. Choose Text | Fonts & Tabs, as in **Figure 2.44**.

2. Choose a monospaced font such as Monaco or Courier, as well as a point size (Monaco 9 is the default).

3. Select a style for your text (Plain is the default).

4. Select the number of spaces you'd like to have between tab stops (5 is the default).

✔ Tip

■ Font and tab settings will be applied globally to all BBEdit documents, not to selected portions of one or more documents.

Changing case:

HTML commands are not case sensitive, but any data that appears in the body of a document is as case sensitive as you'd like it to be. Some HTML authors prefer their code to be in upper or lower case, but usually not in mixed case. BBEdit provides several options that allow you to change the case of a selection of text or an entire document.

1. To change the case of a selection of text, highlight the text to be changed, as in **Figure 2.45**.

2. Select Text | Change Case, which opens the window shown in **Figure 2.46**.

3. Select from the case options and press OK. **Figure 4.47** shows an example of changing the selected text to upper case.

✔ Tip

■ Now you know how to apply case changes to the body of an HTML document. Later in this book, you'll learn to apply case changes to just the HTML tags.

Shifting text to the left or right:

You can shift a text selection one space or one tab stop to the left or right using the Text | Shift Left or Right option. In **Figure 2.48**, for example, I've selected three lines that I'd like to shift to the right.

1. Select the text to be shifted or place the cursor anywhere in a specific line to be shifted.

2. Select Text | Shift Right (or Command+]) to move the text to the right by one tab stop (see **Figure 2.49**).

3. To shift the text one space to the right instead of one tab stop, hold down the Shift key while making the selection.

Figure 2.45 Select the text to which you'd like to apply a change of case.

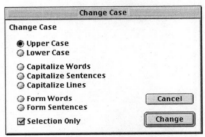

Figure 2.46 From the Change Case menu, select how the case is to be changed.

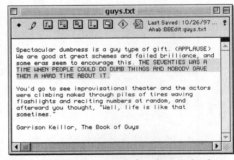

Figure 2.47 The same text after the case has been changed.

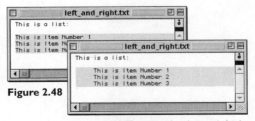

Figure 2.48

Figure 2.49 The text after being shifted to the right by one tab.

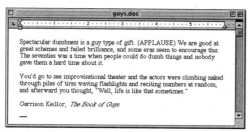

Figure 2.50 BBEdit helps you import data from word processing documents, such as this one from Microsoft Word 6.

Figure 2.51 Word processing documents may contain control characters, called gremlins, that can wreak havoc with your text documents.

Figure 2.52 The Zap Gremlins dialog box.

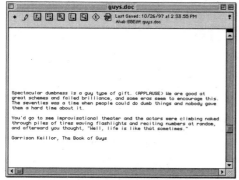

Figure 2.53 A gremlin-free document.

Zapping gremlins:

Word processing programs, such as ClarisWorks and Microsoft Word, rely on complex formatting commands that are stored not as ASCII text but as characters that usually are not understood by pure text editors such as BBEdit. Each word processor has its own way of identifying these formatting commands.

You're likely to encounter gremlins any time you open a document saved as a regular document (rather than as ASCII text or HTML) using a word processor, as in **Figure 2.50**. When you view these documents in an Web browser, you'll see garbage instead of HTML-formatted text, as in **Figure 2.51**. To delete or "zap" gremlins:

1. Select Text | Zap "Gremlins" to open the window shown in **Figure 2.52**.

2. Choose what kinds of gremlins to zap, and what to do with these characters after they've been zapped.

3. Select the Zap button to perform the operation (see **Figure 2.53**).

✔ Tips

- Some gremlins will actually be ASCII text characters themselves, and will therefore be skipped over by this operation. Review the results of the zapping carefully to make sure you deleted everything you intended.

- No ASCII text characters will be deleted by zapping.

MANIPULATING TEXT

Converting tabs and spaces:

The Entab and Detab options under the Text menu allow you to easily convert spaces into tabs (entab) and tabs into spaces (detab). If you're confused about the what this means, think of it in terms of encoding and decoding tabs. This feature is especially useful if you access data from computers running operating systems other than the Mac OS, such as mainframe and mini computers, and the data has been tab- or space-delimited and therefore doesn't line up properly in BBEdit. You may also need to use the Entab and Detab feature when viewing the source code of an HTML document after choosing Save As Text, should you want to cut and paste the code into a new HTML document.

To convert spaces between text into tabs:

1. Highlight the text, as in **Figure 2.54**, where spaces are represented as diamonds and tabs as triangles.

2. Select Text | Entab, which opens the window shown in **Figure 2.55**, and enter the number of spaces to be represented by a tab.

3. Press the Entab button to make the conversion, the results of which are shown in **Figure 2.56**.

To convert tabs into spaces:

1. Highlight the text, as in **Figure 2.57**.

2. Select Text | Detab, which opens the window shown in **Figure 2.58**, and enter the number of spaces to be represented by a tab.

3. Press the Detab button to make the conversion, the results of which are shown in **Figure 2.59**.

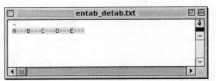

Figure 2.54 To replace spaces with tabs, start by selecting the text containing the spaces.

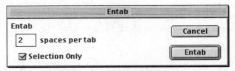

Figure 2.55 Enter the specifics on how you want to make the transformation in the Entab dialog box.

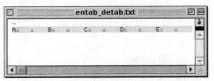

Figure 2.56 The result of applying the Entab command is seen in the triangles, each of which represents a tab stop.

Figure 2.57 To replace tabs with spaces, select the text containing the tabs.

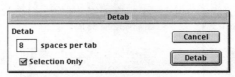

Figure 2.58 Choose the Detab option.

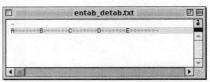

Figure 2.59 The same document with spaces replacing the tabs.

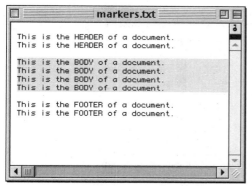

Figure 2.60 To create a marker, start by selecting the area of your document to be identified by a marker.

Figure 2.61 Give your markers easy-to-remember names, like this one.

Figure 2.62 To jump to a section that has been marked, just select it from the Mark menu.

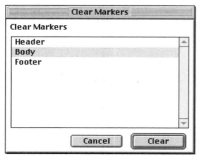

Figure 2.63 Choose the Clear Markers menu to manage a document's markers.

Marking Text

Most HTML documents contain multiple sections of data, and most contain at least three sections:

1. Header
2. Body
3. Footer

BBEdit allows you to select a portion of any document—not just HTML documents—and identify it a section by using markers such as Header, Body, and Footer to define the various sections. You can have as many markers as you like in a document, not just the three mentioned above. Once set, markers make it easy to quickly jump to a particular section of a document, which can save you a lot of time when you have a document that is hundreds of lines long and contains multiple sections.

To set a marker:

1. Select the text to be represented by a marker, as in **Figure 2.60**.

2. Select Mark | Set Marker (or Command+M), which opens the window shown in **Figure 2.61**, and name the marker.

3. Your markers will appear at the bottom of the Mark menu, shown in **Figure 2.62**, where you can easily select them to jump to a particular section.

4. To manage your markers, select Mark | Clear Markers to open the window shown in **Figure 2.63**.

✔ Tips

- Markers have a limited length of about 64 characters. If a marker's name is too long, you'll be prompted to shorten it.

- Holding down the Option key when choosing Command+M will automatically name the section without opening the dialog box.

MARKING TEXT

Spell Checking

BBEdit has a built-in spell checker, but you can use any external spell checker that supports Apple's Word Services Suite, such as Working Software's Spellswell. Check the Spell Checking section of the BBEdit Preferences to select either the internal or an external spell checker (see **Figure 2.64**).

To check the spelling of a document:

1. Select Text | Check Spelling, which opens the window shown in **Figure 2.65**.

2. If you haven't selected any text, your only choice will be Start at Top (as in **Figure 2.64**). Otherwise, your only choice will be Selection Only.

3. Select the Start button and reply to any queries by the spell checker. Your choices are:

   –**Skip All** occurrences of this word.

   –**Add** this entry to the active dictionary.

   –**Replace** the word with a guess or your own entry.

   –**Replace All** occurrences of this word with a guess or your own entry.

   –**Skip** this word.

   –**Cancel** the spell check.

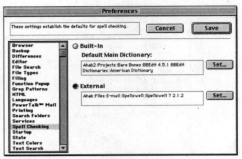

Figure 2.64 You can use an external spell checker, such as Spellswell, as long as it supports Apple's Word Services Suite.

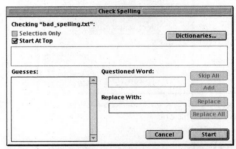

Figure 2.65 BBEdit's built-in spell checker allows you to perform all the tasks associated with a mature spell checker.

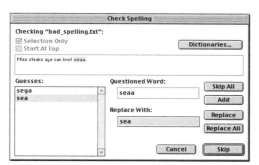

Figure 2.66 BBEdit's spell checker can only detect misspelled words, not incorrect usage of properly spelled words.

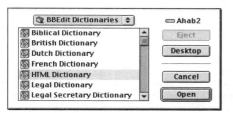

Figure 2.67 You can add dictionaries to BBEdit's spell checker as they become available.

Figure 2.68 If you prefer, you can use an external dictionary, such as Working Software's Spellswell.

To change dictionaries:

1. Start a spell check as usual.

2. Click the Dictionaries button in the upper right-hand corner of the dialog box (as in **Figure 2.66**) to reveal the dictionaries that are currently available.

3. Click the Open button to go to the BBEdit Dictionaries folder shown in **Figure 2.67**), and select an additional dictionary.

To set a default dictionary:

1. Open the BBEdit Preferences by selecting Edit | Preferences (or Command+;).

2. Select the Spell Checking options.

3. Click the Set button in the Default Main Dictionary section and choose the new default dictionary.

✔ Tip

■ External dictionaries such as Spellswell (see **Figure 2.68**) follow their own guidelines when it comes to selecting and adding dictionaries.

SPELL CHECKING

Printing

BBEdit prints documents in pretty much the same way as any other application for the Mac OS. However, your print dialog box will differ depending on the type of printer and the version of print driver installed on your computer.

To print a document:

1. Select File | Print (or Command+P).

2. Press the Print button (see **Figure 2.69**).

To change the printing preferences for a single document:

1. Select File | Print (or Command+P) to print.

2. From the drop-down menu marked General (see **Figure 2.70**), choose BBEdit.

3. Confirm your print options, which are shown in **Figure 2.71**.

To change the printing preferences for all BBEdit documents:

1. Open the BBEdit Preferences by selecting Edit | Preferences (or Command+;).

2. Click on the Printing options (see **Figure 2.72**).

3. Make your printing selections.

Figure 2.69 BBEdit's print dialog box.

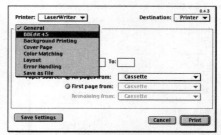

Figure 2.70 To access BBEdit's custom printing options, choose BBEdit 4.5 from the drop-down menu in the print dialog box.

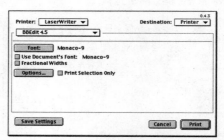

Figure 2.71 You can override several of BBEdit's global settings, such as font and tab settings, as you print an individual document.

Figure 2.72 To configure BBEdit global printing options, choose the Printing section of the BBEdit Preferences window.

3

SEARCHING TEXT

One of BBEdit's greatest strengths is its ability to search and replace text. HTML authors can use BBEdit to find and replace tags and adjust attributes, as well as help maintain entire Web sites. To meet the varying needs of its users, BBEdit provides different levels of searching sophistication, from a no-frills "easy search" to a powerful method of pattern recognition called *grep*.

BBEdit's basic searching features will be familiar to Mac users. You'll easily learn how to search the contents of text and HTML documents for words, tags, character entities (for representing such things as the copyright symbol, ©), and basic formatting commands (such as line breaks and tabs). Once you've found what you're looking for, you can replace it with whatever you like.

Multifile searching lets you search not only the current working document, but an entire folder hierarchy of documents as well. You can even tell BBEdit to search certain types of documents, such as project files, or files whose names end in .htm or .html.

Finally, you can construct highly complex searches using grep, an acronym for *global regular expression and print*. For example, grep will allow you to search a document using the wildcards ? and * to find single and multiple unknown characters, respectively.

Quick Search

The easiest way to locate a simple search string is by using BBEdit's Quick Search feature. This feature allows you to search for one or more characters in a single document, and in real time. In other words, as you type in the Quick Search window (see **Figure 3.1**), the text for which you are searching is automatically highlighted in the body of the document.

To perform a Quick Search:

1. Open a document.

2. Select Windows | Quick Search (or Option+Command+F), as in **Figure 3.2**.

3. Type in the first few characters of the word or text for which you are searching. In this example, I'm searching for the word *Spectacular* (see **Figure 3.3**).

4. As you type characters in the Quick Search window, BBEdit highlights these characters in the body of the document.

✔ Tips

■ The Quick Search will start at the top of the document.

■ By default, searches are case insensitive and will not wrap to the top of the document.

Figure 3.1 Use a Quick Search to look for a simple string of text.

Figure 3.2 Choose Quick Search from the Windows menu to begin a search.

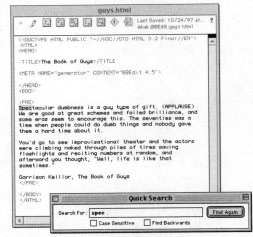

Figure 3.3 Use partial spellings to speed up a search.

QUICK SEARCH

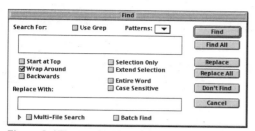

Figure 3.4 The standard Search feature provides much more flexibility for finding text in your documents.

Figure 3.5 Choose Find from the Search menu to begin your search.

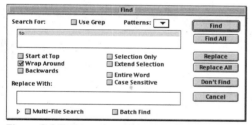

Figure 3.6 Enter regular text or complex grep patterns using the Find command.

Figure 3.7 BBEdit highlights the search term if it's found in the document.

Searching a Single File

For more detailed searching, you'll want to use BBEdit's standard search feature, shown in **Figure 3.4**. There are many aspects to the search feature in BBEdit, including multifile and grep searching, but let's look first at the basics of searching a single file.

To search a single file:

1. Open a document.

2. Select Search | Find (or Command+F), as in **Figure 3.5**.

3. Type in the word or text for which you are searching and click the Find button. In this example, I'm searching for the word *to* (see **Figure 3.6**).

4. BBEdit will close the Find window and highlight the first instance of text in the document that it finds matching your query (see **Figure 3.7**).

5. If no match is found, BBEdit will close the Find window and beep.

As with the Quick Search, BBEdit's Find command starts searching at the top of the document and will stop at the bottom unless you've specified otherwise. The following configuration options are available in the Find window to help you perform a search.

Search options:

- **Start at Top**—forces the search to start at the top of the document every time, even if the cursor is located somewhere else in the active window.

- **Wrap Around**—allows the search to proceed through the end of the document and continue through the beginning of the document up to the the cursor's current location.

- **Backwards**—performs the search from the current cursor position to the top of the document.

- **Selection Only**—searches only the highlighted text (see **Figure 3.8**).

- **Extend Selection**—searches the selected text as well as the rest of the document.

- **Entire Word**—searches for whole words only, no partial words. For example, searching for the word *to* without this option found the word *generator* in line 7 of **Figure 3.7**; with this option selected it will skip on to the first instance of the entire word *to*, as in line 15 of **Figure 3.9**.

- **Case Sensitive**—searches only for instances of the search term that the selected case, such as all capitals, initial capital only, or all lower case. The terms *You* and *you* are not the same when this option is selected.

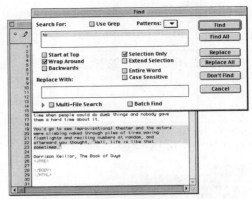

Figure 3.8 You can also search a section of a document instead of the entire document.

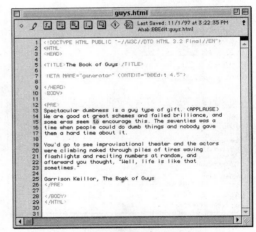

Figure 3.9 You can search for entire words instead of partial words if you think BBEdit will not find your term

Figure 3.10 A Search Results window containing all the "hits" of a search.

Figure 3.11 Save the results of a search for future reference.

Finding All at Once

By default, BBEdit searches one document at a time and for one instance of the search term at a time, but it can search single or multiple documents for all instances of a term at once. This is a useful trick when you need to compare or view how you've used a certain tag in an HTML document. For example, you may need to view how such a tag has been used before you can decide how, or if, it should be replaced.

To simultaneously find and view all instances of a term:

1. Open a document.

2. Select Search | Find (or Command+F) and the enter text for which you are searching.

3. Choose the Find All button.

4. BBEdit will create a new window called Search Results detailing the results.

For example, **Figure 3.10** shows the result of a search for the less-than sign (<), which is used in all HTML tags. The result of this search shows all the lines that contain this tag, as well as the name of the document and the number of the line in which the term appears. By selecting a line in the upper half of the Search Results window, you can view the exact location of the term the lower half of the Search Results window.

✔ Tips

■ You can save the contents of the Search Results window for later review by selecting Save As from the File menu (see **Figure 3.11**).

■ Double-clicking a line in the upper half of the Search Results window (or selecting a line in the upper half of the Search Results window and then clicking Open) brings the document containing that line to the front as the active window.

Replacing Text

Once you've learned how BBEdit searches for text, replacing the text is easy. The "Replace With" field in the lower half of the Find window, shown in **Figure 3.12**, is where you'll enter the replacement text, characters, or tags. For example, if you want to change the formatting of a particular word or words in an HTML document, you can search for the text and replace it with new text or text and HTML tags, as in the example below.

To replace text:

1. Open a document.

2. Select Search | Find (or Command+F) and type in the word or text for which you are searching.

3. Enter the replacement text in the "Replace With" field, as in **Figure 3.12**.

4. Click the Replace button to find and replace the next occurrence of the text, or

5. Click the Replace All button to find and replace all occurrences of the text.

In this example, I've taken a portion of the HTML document, which is the title of a book, and added a bit of HTML code to make the title appear italicized when viewed through a Web browser (see **Figure 3.13**). Choosing the Replace All command would have made this same change to any other occurrences of this text in the document.

✔ Tips

- To undo any changes, even after you have saved the document once the changes have been made, choose Edit | Undo Replace (or Command+Z), shown in **Figure 3.14**.

- To reinstate your changes after undoing them, choose Edit | Redo Replace (or Shift+Command+Z), shown in **Figure 3.15**.

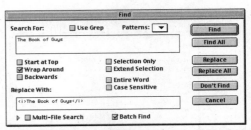

Figure 3.12 Once you've found the text you're looking for, you can replace it with alternative text using the Replace command.

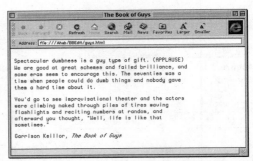

Figure 3.13 The Find and Replace commands work exceptionally well with HTML tags, allowing you to make changes like this in any HTML document.

Figure 3.14 BBEdit will allow you to perform multiple undos if you make mistakes.

Figure 3.15 You can also undo your undos using the Redo Replace command.

REPLACING TEXT

Table 3.1 Special characters that can be used in conjunction with Find and Replace.

Find and Replace Special Characters	
CHARACTER	ACTION
\f	Form feed, also known as a page break.
\n	Line feed, also known as a Unix line break
\t	Tab
\r	Return, also known as a line break

Figure 3.16 Search for and replace spaces, tabs, and blank lines using the Find and Replace commands.

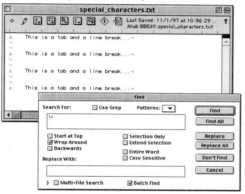

Figure 3.17 Finding and replacing special characters.

Figure 3.18 The result of a find and replace of special characters.

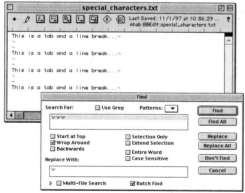

Figure 3.19 Multiple returns are a common problem that can be eliminated using a find and replace.

Searching for Special Characters

You can search and replace special characters in addition to ASCII text and HTML tags. You search and replace these characters just as you do other types of text. The only difference is that you'll be using special characters, including those shown in **Table 3.1**:

To search and replace special characters:

1. Open a document.

2. Select Search | Find (or Command+F) and type in the special characters for which you are searching.

3. Enter the replacement text or other special characters in the "Replace With" field.

4. Click the Replace or Replace All button.

For example, **Figure 3.16** contains four lines of text, each of which begins with a tab and is separated by two blank lines. To remove the tabs, we would execute the find and replace shown in **Figure 3.17**, using \t. The result of the operation is shown in **Figure 3.18**.

To remove the blank lines in **Figure 3.18**, you would execute the find and replace operation shown in **Figure 3.19**, using \r to identify the line returns. The result is shown in **Figure 3.20**.

Figure 3.20 A document after cleaning out unwanted returns.

Searching Multiple Files

By telling BBEdit more about what and where to search, you can search multiple files simultaneously using the Find command. Thus far, we've only been looking at the upper part of the Find command's window. To display the additional Find features associated with multifile searching, click the small triangle to the left of the Multi-File Search checkbox shown in **Figure 3.21** to reveal the features shown in **Figure 3.22**. These additional search parameters include the following:

What

The What option allows you to choose what type of multi-file search to perform (see **Figure 3.23**). BBEdit can search multiple files contained in a folder, a Search Results window, all open BBEdit windows, a Symantec C or C+ or Metrowerks CodeWarrior project, BBEdit group files, or precompiled headers from an external compiler.

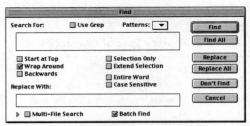

Figure 3.21 Click the triangle beside the Multi-File Search checkbox to reveal BBEdit's advance search features.

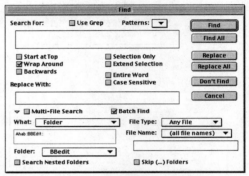

Figure 3.22 Use the Multi-File search capabilities to perform find and replace operations on multiple files.

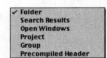

Figure 3.23 Choose what kind of multi-file search to perform.

Searching Multiple Files

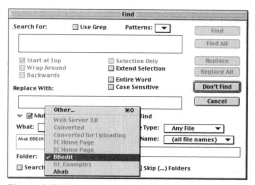

Figure 3.24 Choose a specific folder to search.

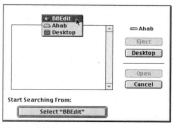

Figure 3.25 Another method of selecting a folder for searching.

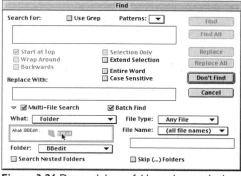

Figure 3.26 Drag and drop a folder to be searched.

Figure 3.27 You can speed up a search by narrowing the type of files you'll be searching.

Folder

The Folder option (see **Figure 3.24**) enables you to select the folder or folder hierarchy to be searched by choosing from the pop-up menu or by selecting Command+0 to identify a folder (see **Figure 3.25**). You can also drag and drop a folder or hard drive icon into the What field to identify the folder to be searched, as in **Figure 3.26**.

File Type

The File Type option allows you to identify what type of file or files are to be searched (see **Figure 3.27**). Narrowing the type of file will improve BBEdit's performance when searching large numbers of files. To search HTML files, choose the Text Files option.

File Name

The File Name option is another way to narrow the search of multiple files. You can select from files that contain or start with certain letters, for example (see **Figure 3.28**). To search only HTML files, try designating only filenames ending with .html.

Additional parameters in the expanded portion of the Find window include

- **Batch Find**—displays the results of a multi-file search in a Search Results window.

- **Search Nested Folders**—continues a multi-file search in any subfolder of the designated search folder.

- **Skip (...) Folders**—during a multi-folder search, skips any folder whose name appears in parentheses ( ).

Finally, when performing a multi-file search and replace, a dialog box like the one shown in **Figure 3.29** will appear asking how you want to dispose of any changes.

Figure 3.28 You can further narrow a search by selecting file-name attributes for searching.

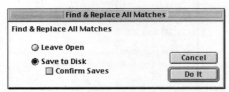

Figure 3.29 BBEdit provides several options to help you save your changes.

Table 3.2 The most commonly used grep commands for BBEdit.

Common Grep Commands for BBEdit	
GREP COMMAND	ACTION
?	A single character (letter or number)
. (period)	A single character (letter or number)
* (asterisk)	Multiple characters (letters or numbers)
#	Any number between 0 and 9
^	Beginning of a line
$	End of a line
[xyz]	Any of the characters x, y, or z, regardless of where they appear within a string of characters
[a-z]	Any character within the range a–z
a|b	Either the character a or b
[aeiou]	Any vowel
[^aeiou]	Any character that isn't a vowel
[a-zA-Z0-9]	Any character (letter or number)
[^aeiou0-9]	Any character other than a vowel or a number
z?	Zero or one z
z*	Zero or more z's
z+	One or more z's

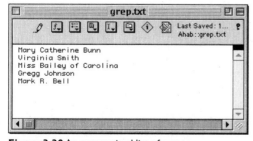

Figure 3.30 An unorganized list of names.

Searching with Grep

The most powerful (and complex) way BBEdit allows you to search and replace text is by using grep patterns. These patterns can be as easy as designating a question mark (?) to represent a single unknown character, as in searching for BB?dit to look for the word BBEdit. Another easy example is using an asterisk (*) to represent multiple unknown characters, as in BB*t to look for BBEdit.

At the other end of the spectrum, however, are the grep patterns that allow you to perform highly complex search-and-replace operations using multiple characters that represent patterns of text. For example, you can use grep to alphabetize rows and columns of text, search and replace dissimilar HTML tags, or search for lines of text that contain the letter Z at the beginning and end of the line.

Grep commands for BBEdit:

Different operating systems and applications support different implementations of grep, so BBEdit's grep commands will not be identical to all other grep commands. However, grep commands tend to be very similar from one system to another, so if you have any grep experience with Nisus Writer or Text Machine for the Mac OS, the grep patterns in **Table 3.1** above or **Table 3.2** below should be familiar.

A simple example:

A simple use of a grep pattern would be to rearrange a list of names from first name first, to last name first. **Figure 3.30** shows a list of five names listed first name first. A grep pattern to reverse this order would look like this:

Search pattern:

^(.*) ([^]+)$

Replace pattern:

\2, \1

The result of applying this grep pattern is shown in **Figure 3.31**. To perform this yourself, follow these steps:

1. Open a new document and type in a few names, each on its own line.

2. Open the Find command by choosing Search | Find (or Command+F).

3. Type the search pattern above into the Search For field (see **Figure 3.32**).

4. Type the Replace pattern into the Replace With field (see **Figure 3.32**)

5. Select the Replace All button.

BBEdit uses parentheses ( ) and brackets [ ] to group patterns, inserting brackets within parentheses to indicate subgroups. In the above example, the search pattern starts with the beginning of line command (^) and ends with the end of line command ($), leaving two groups of commands to be searched.

The replace pattern merely tells BBEdit to replace the second group in place of the first group, after inserting a comma and a blank space between the two groups.

✔ Tips

- Selecting the Replace button instead of the Replace All button instructs BBEdit to find and replace only the first instance of the pattern.

- A grep pattern cannot start with the following characters: (" ? + * '

- If you need to search using one of these grep commands, start the pattern using the caret (^) to indicate the beginning of a line and (.*) to represent multiple unknown characters (see the previous example).

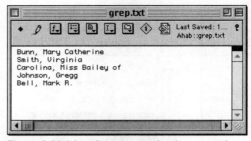

Figure 3.31 A list of names sorted and rearranged using a grep pattern search and replace.

Figure 3.32 A grep search used in conjunction with a replace operation.

Figure 3.33 Grep commands can help manage HTML documents like this one.

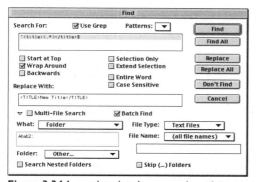

Figure 3.34 A search and replace operation using grep.

Figure 3.35 An HTML document after replacing specific tags using grep.

Practical Grep Examples

Again, BBEdit was originally designed for programmers who could use grep expressions to find and replace highly complex arrangements of computer code. HTML authors can easily take advantage of this feature to manipulate HTML code. The following examples illustrate just how easily this can be accomplished.

Modifying <TITLE> information:

You can use a very basic grep pattern to search and replace an HTML document's title information, regardless of what information exists between the <TITLE></TITLE> tags.

1. Open a new or existing HTML document, such as the one in **Figure 3.33**.

2. Enter the following text in the Search For field (see **Figure 3.34**):

   ^<title>(.*)</title>$

3. Enter the following text in the Replace With field, then select the Replace button:

   <TITLE>New Title</TITLE>

Figure 3.35 shows the result of the grep command.

Modifying a single <BODY> attribute:

You can use grep patterns to modify the following <BODY> attributes in one or more HTML documents:

- bgcolor
- background
- bgsound
- bgproperties
- link
- alink
- vlink
- text

For example, to change the background color of an HTML document from black to white, follow these steps:

1. Open a new or existing HTML document, such as the one in **Figure 3.36**.

2. Enter the following text in the Search For field (see **Figure 3.37**):

   (bgcolor="......")

3. Enter the following text in the Replace With field, then select the Replace button (see Figure 3.37).

   BGCOLOR="FFFFFF"

In this example, BBEdit looks for six unknown letters or numbers enclosed in quotation marks and replaces them with FFFFFF, the hexadecimal equivalent of the color white (see **Figure 3.38**).

✔ Tips

- Unless you select the Case Sensitive checkbox, your Search For data is case insensitive. However, the Replace With data is always case sensitive (see **Figure 3.36**).

Figure 3.36 An HTML document containing <BODY> tag attributes that need correcting.

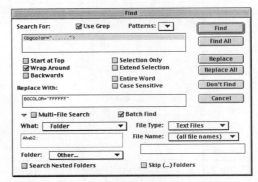

Figure 3.37 Use a grep command to locate six unknown characters in the <BODY> tag, then replace them with new characters.

Figure 3.38 This document will have a different look in a Web browser thanks to grep.

Figure 3.39 A document containing multiple <BODY> tag attributes that need replacing.

Figure 3.40 A more complex example of how to use grep patterns to search and replace HTML data.

Figure 3.41 The result of a grep search and replace.

Modifying multiple <BODY> attributes:

You can also use grep patterns to modify multiple <BODY> attributes, even if they are separated by attributes you don't wish to modify. For example, you may wish to change both the background color and the text color, but not any of the link colors. The following example shows how to perform this type of operation to change the colors of the background and text in a document.

1. Open a new or existing HTML document, such as the one in **Figure 3.39**.

2. Enter the following text in the Search For field (see **Figure 3.40**):

   (bgcolor=". . . . . .") (.*) (text=". . . . . .")

3. Enter the following text in the Replace With field, then select the Replace button (see **Figure 3.40**).

   BGCOLOR="FFFFFF" \2 TEXT="000000"

In this example, BBEdit looks for the BGCOLOR attribute, any unknown characters or letters, then the TEXT attribute, and then replaces only the BGCOLOR and TEXT attributes with the new values (see **Figure 3.41**).

Modifying tags with comments:

As we'll see in the next chapter, one device used by HTML authors to keep track of the many sections of an HTML document is the comment. Web browsers ignore comments, so you can put anything you'd like in a comment and without it appearing in someone's Web browser. With the help of a well-placed comment, you can use a grep search to locate a specific tag even though that tag may appear in several places within the same document.

For example, let's say you have one font size defined for the body of a document, and another font size for links, the header, and the footer of the document. You could use the either of the following comments in conjunction with the <FONT> tag to identify the font size for the body of the document:

```
<!-- BODY FONT -->
<FONT SIZE="+1">
```

...or...

```
<!-- BODY FONT -->
<FONT SIZE="4">
```

To change the font attributes for a commented section and no other:

1. Open a new or existing HTML document.

2. Add a unique comment, such as the one in **Figure 3.42**

3. Enter the following text in the Search For field that incorporates the unique comment (see **Figure 3.43**):

   ```
   <!-- BODY FONT -->\r<FONT SIZE="(.|..)">
   ```

4. Enter the following text in the Replace With field, then select the Replace button (see **Figure 3.43**).

   ```
   <!-- BODY FONT -->\r<FONT SIZE="+3">
   ```

In this example, BBEdit looks for the BODY FONT comment, a hard return, then the FONT SIZE attribute followed by either one or two characters (the FONT SIZE attribute can be modified by 1–7, +1–7, or −1–7). This is an important distinction that grep addresses nicely because it can search using the OR condition. See **Figure 3.44** for the result of this particular use of the grep command.

Figure 3.42 Add a unique HTML comment in conjunction with your tags to be able to use grep more effectively.

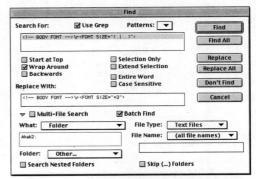

Figure 3.43 A grep search incorporating a predefined search phrase.

Figure 3.44 A document successfully changed using grep.

HTML PRIMER

The two greatest things about the Web are first, that it enables many different types of computers to view complex documents in essentially the same way, and second, that it allows documents and Internet-based services to be hyperlinked to one another. This may not impress you much until you consider that until the Web came along, the best ways for users of different types of computers in different locations around the world to share a document were e-mail and Usenet news—and that meant a plain ASCII text file or binary attachment. Boring!

The Web is a great neutralizer, leveling the playing field for many different types of computers to view and link to documents and online services. This is due largely to HTML, which defines the formatting attributes that allow Web browsers to display information in the same way on many different types of computers.

The biggest limitation to HTML is that it is delineated by an evolving standard that the various Web browsers—Netscape Navigator, Microsoft Internet Explorer, Mosaic, Lynx, and others—implement differently. The consequence is that documents display differently from one browser to the next, which is something you need to take into account when using BBEdit to create HTML documents. The good news, however, is that BBEdit gives you the highest possible degree of control over the final result.

How Does HTML Work?

The process by which HTML documents get from a Web server to a browser is quite simple. HTML is transmitted between Web servers and clients using the Hypertext Transfer Protocol (HTTP), currently at version 1.1. A URL beginning with **http://** instructs your browser to access the server using the HTTP protocol.

When you request an HTML document from a Web server, the response may not be immediate. Depending on the flow of traffic across the network and other factors of data integrity and communication, your document can be delayed at any of the following steps.

Let's sample an HTTP transaction between a Web browser and a typical Web server.

1. The server listens for a connection request.

2. A client sends a request for a document.

3. The server receives the request, which it either accepts or rejects.

4. The server processes the request.

5. The server returns the results of the request.

6. The client receives, processes, and displays the document.

This series of transactions is repeated every time a user clicks a hyperlink in an HTML document or executes a linking command. In addition, every time an HTML document requests an image, the process is repeated. Have you ever noticed that when you request a document with numerous small images, such as little colored balls or icons, it can take a long time to load the entire document? . That's because the browser must submit a new request to the server for every image, and if the HTML document contains numerous images, it can take a really long time to complete loading.

Figure 4.1 Visit the W3C home page for the latest information on HTML standards.

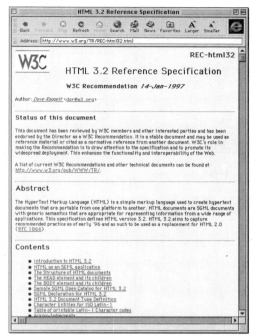

Figure 4.2 The HTML 3.2 reference specification is the best source of information on the proper use of a tag.

Figure 4.3 BBEdit automatically cites HTML 3.2 as a supported version when you create a new document using the HTML Tools palette.

HTML Versions

HTML is categorized by versions much as word processing applications and Web browsers, such as Internet Explorer 3.0.1 and Navigator 4.0.3 are. Each successive version of HTML is typically a superset of the preceding version, with a few minor exceptions along the way. The current version of HTML is 3.2; version 4.0 will be available sometime in 1998.

The group with the most responsibility over deciding what is or is not a part of a particular version of HTML is the World Wide Web Consortium (W3C), which is a joint project of several organizations. For more information on the W3C, visit its home page (shown in **Figure 4.1**) at the following URL:

http://www.w3c.org

HTML is actually a subset of SGML, or Standardized General Markup Language, and is what's known as a Document Type Definition, or DTD. The current HTML 3.2 DTD is very large; if you have any question about the proper use of a tag, you should refer to the HTML 3.2 reference specification (see **Figure 4.2**) at the following URL:

http://www.w3.org/TR/REC-html32.html

BBEdit supports this version of HTML. Every time you create a new document through the HTML Tools palette, you'll notice the following line at the very beginning of the document (see **Figure 4.3**):

<!DOCTYPE HTML PUBLIC "-//W3C//DTD HTML 3.2 Final//EN">

This isn't important to viewers of your documents, but may be important to Web browsers and search engines.

HTML VERSIONS

Basic Tags

The current version of HTML consists of a surprisingly small number of formatting commands, which you use as needed in your HTML documents. The minimal HTML document should contain the following tagging information, usually appearing in pairs often referred to as *tagged pairs*. HTML formatting commands are encased between the less-than (<) and greater-than (>) brackets and typically tell a browser where to start and stop a particular formatting attribute. Other tags, called *stand-alone tags*, are used one at a time. Tags can also appear with attributes and arguments within the opening tag of a tagged pair. Here are the basic HTML formatting tags—all supported by BBEdit—that should be present in all your HTML documents:

```
<!DOCTYPE>
<HTML></HTML>
<HEAD></HEAD>
<TITLE></TITLE>
<BODY></BODY>
```

Rather than residing side-by-side like the pairs in the above example, some tagged pairs should be nested around content. When using nested pairs, it's important to check your document for dangling tags. You'd be surprised by the number of errors caused by authors who forget to close a tagged pair with a concluding tag! Here are the tags that determine the basic structure of an HTML document, which you can see when you choose New Document from the HTML Tools palette (see **Figure 4.4**)

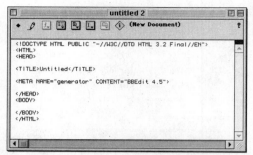

Figure 4.4 Use the HTML Tools palette to create a new HTML document.

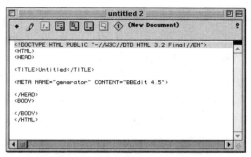

Figure 4.5 The <!DOCTYPE> tag is used to identify what type of document you have created, as well as what version of HTML it supports.

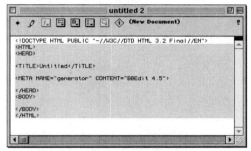

Figure 4.6 The <HTML></HTML> tag will contain most all of your Web page's information.

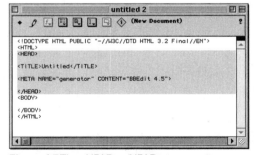

Figure 4.7 The <HEAD></HEAD> tag contains information used to identify a document by title as well as comments and META data.

<!DOCTYPE>

The <!DOCTYPE> tag (see **Figure 4.5**) indicates in what version of HTML the document has been created. Not all Web servers and browsers use this information.

<HTML></HTML>

The <HTML> tag denotes the beginning of an HTML document and the </HTML> tag concludes the document (see **Figure 4.6**). Naturally, these tags do not appear together; all other information in your HTML document will be nested between these two tags.

<HEAD></HEAD>

Data within the <HEAD></HEAD> tags (see **Figure 4.7**) contains descriptive information about an HTML document, including the title and any comments the author may wish to insert regarding the content, location, and purpose of the document, for example. These comments are not read by the browser, but anyone who saves the document as a text file can view them manually. Here is an example of a comment that has been broken into several short lines:

```
<HTML>
<HEAD>
<!--Created 11/1/97-->
<!--Last edited 11/10/97-->
<!--Author: mbell@ncha.org-->
```

BASIC TAGS

<TITLE></TITLE>

Nested between the <HTML> and <HEAD> tags is the <TITLE></TITLE> tagged pair (see **Figure 4.8**). The title you give you document should be short and to the point for several reasons. First, many browsers, such as Netscape Navigator, use the information in the <TITLE></TITLE> to name the bookmark created from your document; this information also appears in the title bar of your browser. Failure to give your document a title might result in the filename of your document appearing in the title bar as well as in your bookmarks. You can also place META data within these tags, such as keywords and descriptions, which provide information for search engines (as in **Figure 4.8**).

<BODY></BODY>

Everything not contained in the header belongs in the <BODY></BODY> section of your document (see **Figure 4.9**). This includes all text, images, and hyperlinks in your document.

The closing </BODY> tag should always be the next to the last tag in your document.

✔ Tips

■ HTML ignores not only blank lines but all white space, so as far as the browser is concerned, you could place a blank line between each word of text without changing your document. Likewise, an HTML document could be one long sentence and again you would see the same result in the browser.

■ HTML documents should be as concise and to the point as possible without sacrificing grace and clarity. I recommend writing your HTML documents with as little white space as possible; nesting your tags as in the example above is completely optional. Do what works for you, but be consistent.

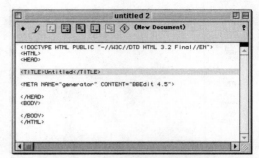

Figure 4.8 The title of you document goes here, which appears in the status bar area of a Web browser.

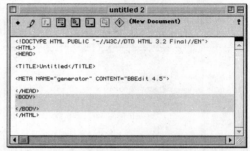

Figure 4.9 The body of a document is where all your substantive information will be located.

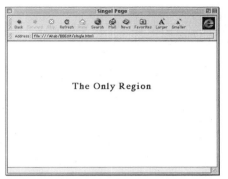

Figure 4.10 An HTML document with one region for text and images.

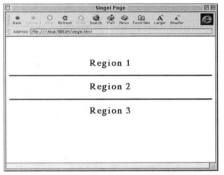

Figure 4.11 HTML documents can be divided into regions using dividers such as horizontal rules.

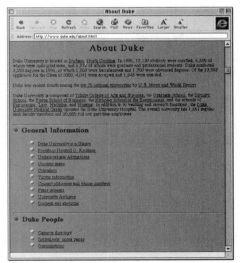

Figure 4.12 Many Web sites still use a single region for their main Web pages.

Layout Options

HTML documents may be laid out in any of several ways, although HTML doesn't provide nearly as many layout options as do most word processors (Microsoft Word or ClarisWorks, for example) or page-layout applications (such as QuarkXPress or Adobe PageMaker). As HTML standards improve, more layout options will become available. For now, you have only four basic options:

- single region
- tables
- frames
- columns

These basic layout options determine how a page is divided into regions. Early versions of HTML only allowed for a single page layout. Today most Web sites employ a mixture of these layout options, and some include several on the same page. Each layout style has its advantages and disadvantages. Deciding whether to use one or more style in your HTML documents is a matter of personal taste.

Single Region

A single-region layout is the most common format used in first-generation HTML documents (see **Figure 4.10**). This format is composed of a page with a single region for content. In second-generation HTML documents that content is divided with horizontal rules (lines) and thin horizontal images (see **Figure 4.11**).

This type of layout is still popular for several reasons, including ease of creation and maintenance. It's ideal for long documents that don't require complex formatting. **Figure 4.12** is a good example of this type of layout.

Tables

The advent of tables has had a dramatic impact on the way HTML documents are designed, because tables allow you to break a document into multiple regions (see **Figure 4.13**). They can be used to mimic spreadsheets featuring evenly spaced rows and columns, such as those produced with ClarisWorks, Microsoft Excel, or Lotus 1-2-3. Or they can be used to create highly complex Web pages like the one shown in **Figure 4.14**. The individual cells of a table can be populated with formatted text, images, multimedia objects such as movies, or blank space for balancing your page design. The result is a tremendous improvement in the flexibility of layout possibilities when compared to earlier versions of HTML.

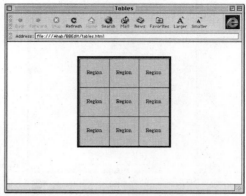

Figure 4.13 Tables allow HTML authors to divide Web pages into multiple regions.

Figure 4.14 A large percentage of Web sites use tables to create highly complex presentations.

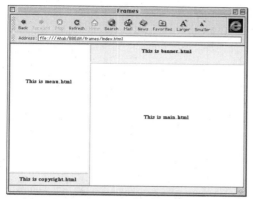

Figure 4.15 Frames offer a different type of control over page layout.

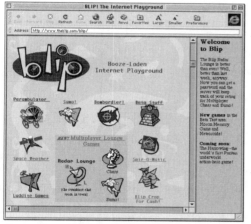

Figure 4.16 Rob Terrell's Web site, The Blip, uses frames to divide instructions and online games into two independent areas.

Frames

Frames add yet another dimension to HTML document layout by dividing a Web browser window into multiple regions, each controlled by a separate HTML document. In **Figure 4.15**, for example, a single document called index.html points to four additional HTML documents, each of which appears in a separate frame:

menu.html
copyright.html
banner.html
main.html

Frames can be a bit trickier to use than tables, but they add one important capability that all the other layout options don't provide—the freedom to click in one frame and have a resulting action occur in one of the other frames while leaving the remaining frames unchanged. This allows you to display static information in one frame while dynamic information displays at the same time have in one or more additional frames. See **Figure 4.16** for an example of a very well-implemented site by Rob Terrell using frames.

Columns

You can use the final layout option, columns, to achieve an effect similar to tables and frames. Currently columns work only with Netscape Navigator, but future versions of other browsers may support columns as well. **Figure 4.17** shows an example of columns in an HTML document.

In an HTML document, columns work much the same way as in popular word processing applications. You can define the number of columns you want to display, as well as the space between columns and the overall width of the set of columns. As most newspapers and magazines are laid out using columns, this layout option is especially useful for online magazines (see **Figure 4.18**).

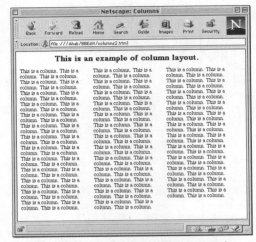

Figure 4.17 Netscape Navigator offers support for columns, which is yet another approach to page layout in HTML.

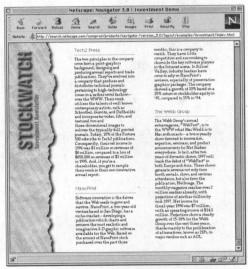

Figure 4.18 This sample newsletter uses columns to make reading easier on the eye.

Table 4.1

Hyperlinking Options	
ACCESS PROTOCOL	LINKS TO...
file	A local or remote text file for viewing.
ftp	A file on a remote ftp server for downloading.
gopher	Files on a remote Gopher server.
http	Local or remote HTML documents.
mailto	Internet e-mail using SMTP.
news	Usenet newsgroup articles.
telnet	A Telnet service.

Figure 4.19 You can use text-based hyperlinks in your HTML documents to link to other documents or Internet-based services.

Figure 4.20 Most Web sites will use images as hyperlinks as well.

Hyperlinking Options

Hyperlinking is essential to how the Web works, and there are many ways you can go about implementing hyperlinks in your HTML documents. You can link to a location within the same document or to another document entirely by clicking on text or an image, or you can link to the following types of Internet-based servers by specifying one of several types of access protocols at the appropriate place within a URL (see **Table 4.1**).

The mechanics of creating a hyperlink to another document or service are very similar. For example, the following code is used to create the textual hyperlink shown in **Figure 4.19**:

```
<A HREF=http://www.barebones.com>Bare Bones home page</a>
```

Adding an image as the hyperlink is just as easy, as in the following code:

```
<A HREF=http://www.barebones.com><IMG SRC="bbedit_badge1.gif"></A>
```

Figure 4.20. shows how the image hyperlink looks through a Web browser.

Table **4.2** shows an example of each of the access protocols listed in **Table 4.1** above when they're used to create a URL:

So, once you have a URL, you can link it to some text or an image to create a hyperlink. **Table 4.3** shows an example of each of the previous URLs converted into hyperlinks.

Figure 4.21 shows how these hyperlinks are displayed through a Web browser.

Table 4.2

Access Protocols as URLs

ACCESS PROTOCOL	EXAMPLE URL
file	file:///<local hard drive>filename.html
ftp	ftp://ftp.barebones.com/
gopher	gopher://gopher.mtsu.edu
http	http://www.barebones.com/
mailto	mailto:bailey@barebones.com
news	news:comp.infosystems
telnet	telnet://ducatalog.lib.duke.edu

Table 4.3

Examples of Hyperlinks

ACCESS PROTOCOL	EXAMPLE URL
file	\<A HREF="file:///filename.htm"> Local file</a>
ftp	\<A HREF="ftp://ftp.barebones.com"> FTP server</A>
gopher	\<A HREF="gopher://gopher.mtsu.edu"> Gopher server</A>
http	\<A HREF="http://www.barebones.com/"> Web server</A>
mailto	\<A HREF="mailto:bailey@barebones.com" E-mail server</A>
news	\<A HREF="news:comp.infosystems"> Usenet news server</A>
telnet	\<A HREF="telnet://ducatalog.lib.duke.edu"> Telnet server</A>

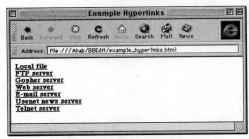

Figure 4.21 Here's how the hyperlinks in Table 4.3 look when viewed through a Web browser.

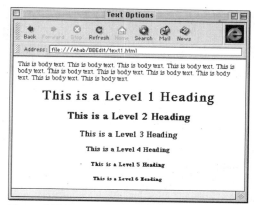

Figure 4.22 First-generation HTML documents offered limited text-formatting options.

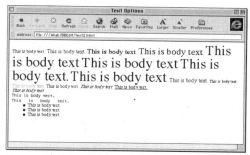

Figure 4.23 The text-formatting options available today in HTML 3.2 are starting to rival those of popular word processing applications.

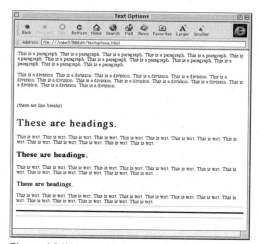

Figure 4.24 You can also use several different HTML tags to divide text into sections within the same page.

Text Options

HTML 3.2 offers many options for formatting text, an essential element of HTML. In the early days of the Web, we had very limited options when it came to text formatting: plain body text and six levels of headings were the most commonly used formatting options (see **Figure 4.22**). Subsequent versions of HTML have provided additional possibilities, including relative size, color, and alignment (see **Figure 4.23**).

Text can now be divided into sections using several different HTML tags (as opposed to page layout options), such as the following (see **Figure 4.24**):

- <P></P> (paragraph)
- <DIV></DIV> (divisions)
-
 (line breaks)
- <H></H> (headings)
- <HR> (horizontal rules)

Text formatting is probably the most important part of creating well-defined HTML documents. Chapter 5, "HTML Tools" explores all of BBEdit's capabilities in this area.

Image Options

Images have always been an important part of HTML, and almost no Web site should be without plenty of them. Images serve many purposes, despite the few purists out there who tend to shy away from including them in their HTML documents. In fact, there are Web browsers still in use that are incapable of viewing images at all. For example, **Figure 4.25** shows the Bare Bones home page viewed through one of these, MacLynx; **Figure 4.26** shows the same page viewed through a browser that is capable of displaying images.

Images can be used for many purposes, including

- backgrounds
- hyperlinks
- navigation
- decoration
- advertisement
- content

Most images will be incorporated into an HTML document as a background image or an inline image. Background images are used by most Web browsers in place of a background color (such as gray or white), allowing you to create more colorful documents. BBEdit easily supports the use of background images, an example of which looks like this within the HTML document:

`<BODY BACKGROUND="rocks.jpg">`

Figure 4.27 shows how this particular example looks in a Web browser.

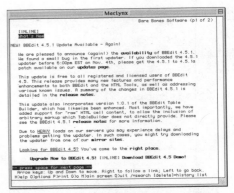

Figure 4.25 Some people use text-only Web browsers like MacLynx, which are unable to display images.

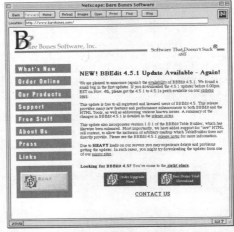

Figure 4.26 Here's how the Web page shown in the previous figure looks when viewed through an image-capable Web browser.

Figure 4.27 When used as backgrounds, images provide a whole new realm to Web page design.

Figure 4.28 Images may be effectively used as client- and server-side clickable image maps, which allows a single image to link to multiple locations using "hot-spots" to identify a specific target URL.

Figure 4.29 Client-side image maps require about the same amount of code as server-side image maps, but not a CGI program to operate them.

Inline images may be used as static objects or, as we've seen above (see **Figure 4.20**), as clickable hyperlinked objects that can take viewers to another document or Internet-based service. A clickable image can be either a single-purpose image or an image that contains multiple "hotspots" that link to different targets.

These images are known as clickable image maps, and they come in two varieties:

1. server-side image maps

2. client-side image maps

A server-side image map requires that a program called a Common Gateway Interface (CGI) be running on the Web server to interpret your mouse clicks, whereas a client-side image map can interpret the mouse clicks on its own. **Figure 4.28**, for example, shows a client-side image map that uses a single image file capable of linking to several other documents without the aid of a CGI program. **Figure 4.29** shows what the code looks like that's used to allow this type of capability.

IMAGE OPTIONS

HTML Tools

The heart of BBEdit's HTML authoring ability lies in the HTML Tools, a series of plug-ins created by Lindsay Davies and Jim Correia that help you create and manipulate HTML data with ease. HTML versions are constantly changing, and BBEdit's plug-in architecture provides the opportunity for programmers to add features to BBEdit without requiring that the entire program be rewritten to include them.

Version 4.5.1 of BBEdit comes with more than two dozen HTML Tools that can be accessed in a variety of ways—through floating palettes, pull-down menus, AppleScripts, Frontier scripts, and macros. You can easily record your own macros and scripts to create your own tools. And, in addition to the HTML Tools, BBEdit includes an assortment of other plug-ins; we'll explore them in Chapter 8. In short, BBEdit offers much more flexibility than you'll find in other HTML authoring tools.

The drawback is that with so many HTML Tools and so many ways to access them, it takes a bit of work to remember all the tools and how to use them. This chapter shows you what you need to know to start using the BBEdit HTML Tools, and then explores them according to their position in the Tools menu.

Getting Started

Before you can use all the features of BBEdit's HTML Tools, you'll need to go into the Preferences and make a few configuration choices first.

To configure BBEdit's HTML Preferences:

1. Choose Edit | Preferences (or Command+;) to open the Preferences window.

2. Choose the HTML options (see **Figure 5.1**)

3. Select whether you want your HTML tags to be in upper or lower case.

4. Enter the name of your Web server (if necessary).

5. Enter the path to your default HTML documents directory (if necessary).

6. Enter the default filename for your server's documents (usually index.html, default.html, or home.html).

7. Locate the local default directory in which BBEdit will find your HTML documents (if necessary).

8. Locate the local default directory in which BBEdit can find your HTML templates (if necessary).

9. Select the Text options window (see **Figure 5.2**).

10. Select the colors you want to use for general, anchor, and image tags.

11. Press the Save button to save your options and exit the Preferences window.

✔ Tips

■ Changes to BBEdit's Preferences will go into effect immediately.

■ See Appendix B for more details on all the BBEdit Preferences.

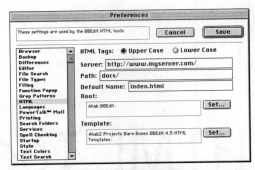

Figure 5.1 Configuring your HTML Preferences before getting down to work is the first step.

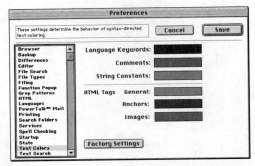

Figure 5.2 Choose the default or your own colors to make working with HTML code easier on the eye.

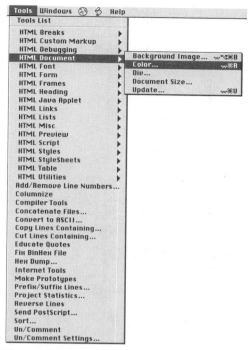

Figure 5.3 Using the Tools menu to access BBEdit's HTML Tools is one of three ways to access the Tools.

Figure 5.4 The BBEdit Tools palette is another way to access the HTML Tools.

Configuring the HTML Tools Palette

There are three main ways to access BBEdit's HTML Tools. Generally speaking, this type of variety is a good thing, as it allows some people to use the floating palette, for example, while others might prefer using the pull-down menu instead. The downside is that these methods of access are not organized in the same way, which can lead to confusion if you try switching back and forth between them.

To access the HTML Tools:

1. Choose a tool from the Tools pull-down menu (see **Figure 5.3**), or

2. Choose a tool from the BBEdit Tools floating palette (see **Figure 5.4**), or

3. Choose a tool from the HTML Tools floating palette (see **Figure 5.5**).

You can get an idea from these examples how accessing the same tool (selecting an HTML document color) can be done in three different ways. The options presented in the Tools menu are identical to those in the BBEdit Tools palette, but the HTML Tools palette is very different because it is highly configurable.

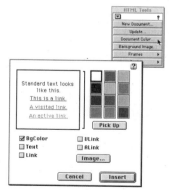

Figure 5.5 The HTML Tools palette offers customizable access to the same Tools as do the Tools menu and BBEdit Tools palette.

Configuring the HTML Tools palette:

You can configure the HTML Tools palette in several ways to suit your needs. For example, you can choose to hide the palette and rely on the pull-down menu or the BBEdit Tools palette for access to the tools instead.

Or, you can customize the palette to display only the buttons you use on a regular basis, as well as define wide/narrow or thick/thin buttons, depending on how you prefer to view them.

1. To toggle between a collapsed and expanded view of the palette, click the key in **Figure 5.6**.

2. To configure how the palette appears on screen, including the shape and number of buttons to be displayed, choose Configure Buttons from the drop-down menu at the top of the HTML Tools palette (see **Figure 5.7**).

3. To select the buttons you want to appear in the palette, highlight them and click the OK button.

4. To remove a button from the palette, highlight the item while holding down the Command key, then click the OK button.

✔ Tips

■ The difference between choosing an item from the palette versus the pull-down menu is negligible.

■ The pull-down menu groups the tools in a more logically than does the palette.

Figure 5.6 Click the key in the HTML Tools palette to collapse and expand the palette window.

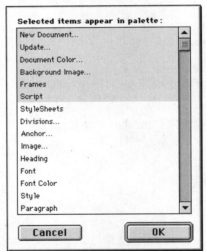

Figure 5.7 The HTML Tools palette is highly configurable.

Figure 5.8 The Breaks menu is where you'll go to insert several different kinds of breaks.

Figure 5.9 The horizontal rule is one of the most commonly used breaks, and can be customized.

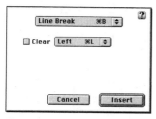

Figure 5.10 Line breaks have similar options to the horizontal rules, but perform a different function.

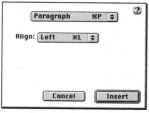

Figure 5.11 You may either insert a paragraph tag, or highlight a word, sentence, or paragraph and surround it with a pair of paragraph tags.

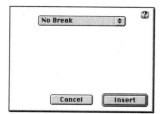

Figure 5.12 The <NOBR> tag prevents text from being wrapped in a browser window.

Breaks

The Breaks tools (see **Figure 5.8**) provide multiple options that allow you to break the flow of text in a document. Use these options by inserting the cursor where the break is to be placed, or highlight the text that is to be surrounded by the tags (<P>here is some text</P>).

To insert a break:

1. Choose the Options submenu to manually select one of the Break options from a pop-up list and configure that tag's attributes. Otherwise, the tag's default attributes will be automatically inserted.

2. Choose Horizontal Rule (see Figure 5.9) to insert a horizontal rule with the value of <HR SIZE="0">.

3. Choose Line Break (see Figure 5.10) to insert a line break with the value of <BR>.

4. Choose Paragraph Break (see **Figure 5.11**) to insert a paragraph mark with the value of <P>...</P>.

5. Choose No Break (see **Figure 5.12**) to insert a non-breaking mark with the value of <NOBR>...</NOBR>.

6. Choose Word Break (see **Figure 5.13**) to insert a word break directly after the selected word or after the insertion point with the value of <WBR>.

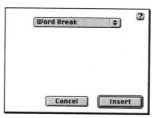

Figure 5.13 To break a line of text into two or more lines, insert the <WBR> tag.

BREAKS

Custom Markup

The Custom Markup tool (see **Figure 5.14**) allows you to write and save macros as BBEdit plug-ins. For example, you can write a custom macro that takes the selected text and applies custom HTML formatting, such as increasing the relative font size.

To create a custom markup macro:

1. Choose the Custom Markup option from the Tools menu.

2. Select a macro to edit, or choose one of the "Undefined" macros for editing and then rename it (see **Figure 5.15**).

3. From the drop-down menu to the left, choose from the many predefined actions as the basis of the macro (see **Figure 5.16**). In this example, the macro simply takes the selected text and applies a custom <FONT> tag with attributes.

4. Choose the Save Plug-In button to save the macro as a BBEdit Plug-in (see **Figure 5.17**), which will be available the next time you launch BBEdit.

5. Click the Done button when you've finished the macro, and the Execute button to execute the macro (see **Figure 5.18**).

In this example, the following is the result of the custom markup macro after highlighting the text "Here is some text."

<FONT SIZE=+1>Here is some text.</FONT>

Figure 5.14 The Custom Markup Tool allows you to create your own HTML formatting tool using a macro.

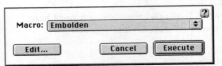

Figure 5.15 BBEdit comes with one predefined macro called Embolden, which makes the selected text bold.

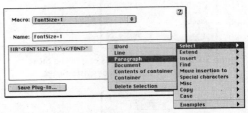

Figure 5.16 To create your own macro, select the pop-down triangle and choose from one or more of the many macro commands.

Figure 5.17 Choosing the Save As Plug-in button allows you to save the macro as a BBEdit Plug-in, which will be stored in the BBEdit Plug-ins folder.

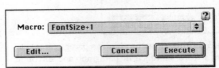

Figure 5.18 Once saved as a plug-in or custom macro, your new tools will be available in the Custom Markup Tool menu.

CUSTOM MARKUP

Figure 5.19 The Debugging menu provides shortcuts to several helpful tools that assist you in checking and organizing your documents.

Figure 5.20 The Balance Tags Tool helps locate the closest pair of tags.

Figure 5.21 The Check HTML Tool is one of the most valuable of all the HTML Tools.

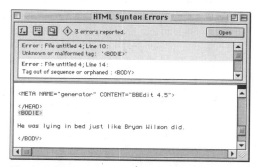

Figure 5.22 The report generated by the Check HTML Tool provides you with detailed information on your document in a familiar interface.

Debugging

The Debugging tools (see **Figure 5.19**) provide several ways to help you check the tags and links of your documents for errors.

To check for balanced tags:

The Balance Tags tool selects the text and pair of tags closest to the insertion point to help you verify that you have properly used the pair of tags (see **Figure 5.20**).

1. Select Balance Tags from the Debugging submenu to find the closest pair of tags.

2. Repeat this process to move outward and locate the next pair of balanced (i.e., same) tags.

To check HTML code for errors:

The Check HTML tool (see **Figure 5.21**) allows you to review a document for HTML 3.2 standardization. This tool isn't perfect when it comes to reviewing highly customized HTML documents, but it will report errors even though your documents appear properly in a Web browser, and it helps you write better documents by finding basic errors.

1. Select Check HTML from the Debugging submenu.

2. If your code appears OK, a message will appear to this effect. If not, a debugging report like the one shown in **Figure 5.22** will appear telling you where the apparent errors are located.

DEBUGGING

To check hyperlinks for errors:

The Check Links tool searches the folder you've identified in your BBEdit Preferences as the root folder and verifies that any links to these documents in your current working document are valid. Note: This option will not check documents over the Web or on another server.

1. Select Check Links from the Debugging submenu.

2. If your links appears OK, a message will appear to this effect. If not, a debugging report like the one shown in **Figure 5.23** will appear telling you where the apparent errors are located.

3. Select the Check Links Options to configure how errors are reported.

4. Select Check Site Links from the Debugging submenu to review all the documents in your root folder. See **Figure 5.24** for an example error report.

To format the nesting of your tags:

The Format tool rearranges the way your tags are nested to help you identify orphaned tags and other errors. You can use this tool not only to debug your code, but also to make it look more appealing!

1. Select Format from the Debugging submenu and choose the format that you prefer (see **Figure 5.25**).

2. Your document will then be rearranged according to the selected pattern (see **Figure 5.26**).

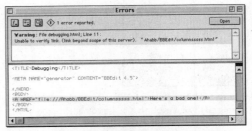

Figure 5.23 The Check Links debugging tool checks for broken links on your local file system.

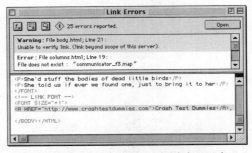

Figure 5.24 If your document contain links to other servers, they will not be checked.

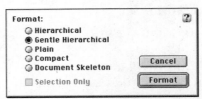

Figure 5.25 Use the Format tool to rearrange how your tags are formatted.

Figure 5.26 The Format tool can rearrange your tags in a nested fashion for easier reading.

DEBUGGING

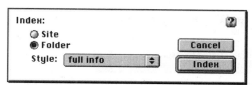

Figure 5.27 The Index Site tool can quickly create an HTML document that lists all the other documents in a folder or on your entire document root folder.

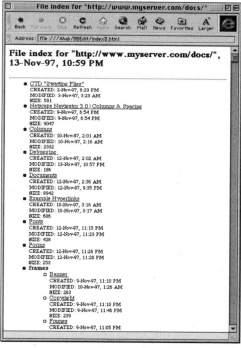

Figure 5.28 A sample index created by the Site Index tool.

Indexing your documents:

One of the most helpful HTML Tools is the Index Site tool, which catalogs the contents of your root document folder and creates an HTML document that summarizes its contents.

1. Select Index Site from the Debugging submenu.

2. In the Index option window (see **Figure 5.27**), choose a format that you prefer, such as a full index of the contents of your entire document root folder.

3. BBEdit will create an index like the one shown in **Figure 5.28**, which you'll need to name and save.

DEBUGGING

Document

The Document tools (see **Figure 5.29**) provide shortcuts to several miscellaneous attributes of HTML documents, including background image and color control.

Selecting a background image:

BBEdit makes it easy to add background images, which add depth and flexibility to HTML documents.

1. Select Background Image from the Document submenu.

2. Select an image file (see **Figure 5.30**) and indicate whether you want the path to this document to be relative, to include the entire path to your document root folder, or to have the full path as it will appear once uploaded to your Web server (i.e., http://www...).

✔ Tips

- Small images are best for background images.

- The fewer colors in your background images, the faster they will load in a Web browser.

Figure 5.29 Use the Document tools to format and arrange sections within documents.

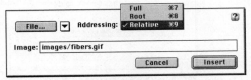

Figure 5.30 The Background Image option makes inserting background images a snap.

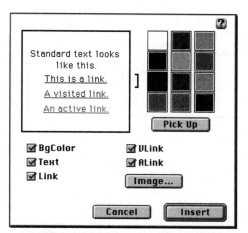

Figure 5.31 Use the Color tool to select font colors for all aspects of a document, including links and background colors.

Selecting document colors:

BBEdit allows you to control the following color elements in an HTML document through the Color tool:

- background
- text
- links
- visited links
- active links

You can also use the Color tool to select background images (see the previous section for more information).

1. Select Color from the Document submenu (see **Figure 5.31**)

2. Select the checkboxes beside the elements you want to define.

3. Select the colors for these elements by selecting from the color swatches.

✔ Tips

- Double-clicking on a color will open the Mac OS's color picker, where you can redefine a color.

- Select the Pick Up button to redefine the color swatches to reflect the colors that are currently in use by the document.

DOCUMENT

Dividing a document into logical sections:

You can use the Div tool to divide your HTML documents into logical sections, as well as apply alignment attributes such as centering a paragraph.

1. Select a word, line, or paragraph of text with the mouse.

2. Select Div from the Document submenu (see **Figure 5.32**)

3. Give the division a name and an alignment attribute, then select the Insert button.

The resulting division will appear as a paragraph of running text.

Determining a document's size:

You can use the Document Size tool to evaluate the size of your HTML document and its images. This tells you the total size of the document as it will be loaded by a Web browser with inline image loading enabled, and helps determine how long it might take visitors to load your documents.

1. Select Document Size from the Document submenu.

2. BBEdit will calculate your document's size and display it in a modal window (see **Figure 5.33**).

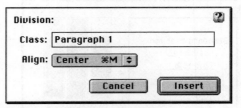

Figure 5.32 You can divide documents into sections to make them easier to manage.

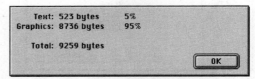

Figure 5.33 Determine the total size of a document and its inline images by using the Document Size tool.

DOCUMENT

Figure 5.34 Updating placeholders and includes for all the HTML documents on an entire Web site.

Updating placeholders and includes:

The Update tool updates *placeholders* and *includes*, which are discussed in detail in the next chapter. In brief, placeholders and includes are shorthand substitutes for information such as the title of an HTML document, which is represented as #TITLE#.

1. Select Update from the Document submenu.

2. Select an option to either update the current document or an entire site.

3. Click the Update button (see **Figure 5.34**).

Font

The HTML Font tools apply formatting to selected text, including size and color attributes. You can select a specific size from the HTML Font menu (see **Figure 5.35**), or you can select the Options menu and define the attributes more precisely. For example, **Figure 5.36** shows the Font options, and **Figure 5.37** shows the Base Font options.

To change font size:

1. Highlight the text you'd like to resize.

2. Select the size (+1–7) or Options from the HTML Font submenu.

3. To reduce the size of a font, you must select the Options menu.

To change font color:

1. Highlight the text you'd like to color.

2. Select Font Color from the HTML Font submenu (see **Figure 5.38**).

3. Select one of the 12 predefined colors, or double-click on one of the colors to use the Mac OS's color picker to change the color.

To change to small caps:

The Small Caps option changes text into all upper case, then takes the first letter of each word and makes it two points larger than the others, as in **Figure 5.39**.

1. Highlight the text you'd like to change.

2. Select Small Caps from the HTML Font submenu.

Figure 5.35 The HTML Font tools submenu.

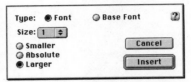

Figure 5.36 The first half of the Font Options tool is where you'll configure regular font options.

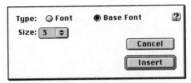

Figure 5.37 The second half of the Font Options tool is where you'll configure base font options.

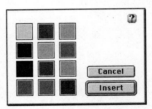

Figure 5.38 Use the Font Color option to select either a predefined or a custom font color.

Figure 5.39 The Small Caps option converts all letters of a selection into upper case, then increases the size of the initial letter.

Figure 5.40 The HTML Form tool allows you to insert rudimentary information relating to forms, but not any of the form elements.

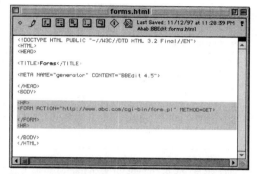

Figure 5.41 The beginning of a form entry in an HTML document.

Form

Most Web sites are like one-way streets because visitors can receive, but not send, data. Forms, and the programs that run them called Common Gateway Interfaces (CGIs), allow users to send data to a Web server. If you've used a search engine like AltaVista or Yahoo, then you've used a form to enter your search queries. Programmers can use BBEdit to write these CGIs in languages such as Perl and C++, but HTML authors can also use BBEdit to help create the forms that users will need to use these CGIs.

To insert a URL to a CGI:

Every form must reference a CGI in the same way that most other URLs reference a target as part of a hyperlink. CGIs can understand three commands: GET, HEAD, and POST. Because the HEAD command is rarely used, BBEdit doesn't include it as part of the HTML Form tool.

1. Place the cursor where you'd like to insert the form.

2. Select Options from the HTML Form submenu (see **Figure 5.40**).

3. Decide whether your form requires the GET or POST method and make the appropriate selection.

4. Select the Rules checkbox if you'd like to encase your form data in horizontal rules.

5. Type in the URL to the CGI, or use the drop-down triangle to locate the file on your local hard drive.

6. Click the Insert button, the result of which is shown in **Figure 5.41**.

✔ Tip

■ The current version of HTML Tools doesn't support the creation of form elements, such as check boxes, text input fields, and radio buttons.

FORM

Frames

The HTML Frames tool (see **Figure 5.42**) gives BBEdit users the ability to create frames, discussed in the previous chapter. A framed page consists of three main components—a frameset, frames, and comments for browsers that aren't capable of viewing frames.

To create a frameset:

1. Create a new document to serve as the frame index page.

2. Choose Frameset from the HTML Frames tool menu (see **Figure 5.43**) and enter the row heights or column widths for the frameset.

3. Choose Frame from the HTML Frames tool menu (see **Figure 5.44**) and enter the information required to identify each frame. Repeat this step for each frame.

4. Save the document (as in **Figure 5.45**) and open it in a frame-compliant Web browser (see **Figure 5.46**).

✔ Tips

■ Framed pages can have multiple framesets, including a mix of frame rows and columns.

■ Use the No frames tool to enter comments for users who cannot view frames.

■ Frames can be tricky to successfully incorporate into a Web site, so use them with caution.

Figure 5.42 The HTML Frames tool menu.

Figure 5.43 To get started, use the Frameset tool first, even though it appears second in the menu.

Figure 5.44 The Frame option is where you'll identify a different HTML document for each frame panel.

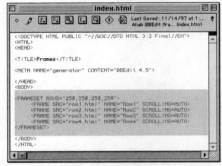

Figure 5.45 A four-frame sample document.

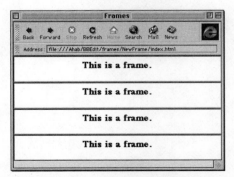

Figure 5.46 The sample document seen in Internet Explorer.

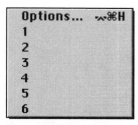

Figure 5.47 The HTML Heading tool menu.

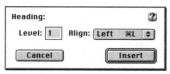

Figure 5.48 Choose the Options menu to customize a heading, including size and alignment.

Figure 5.49 A sample document containing all size and alignment possibilities.

Heading

HTML 3.2 supports six levels of headings, level one being the largest font size and level six the smallest. You can use the HTML Heading tool (see **Figure 5.47**) to enter one of these head tags with a default left alignment, or choose the Options submenu choice to change the alignment and level of a heading.

To apply a heading:

1. Select the text you want to convert into a heading.

2. Select 1-6 from the HTML Heading submenu to accept the default left-alignment.

3. Or, to customize a heading, choose Options instead and customize the heading (see **Figure 5.48**).

Figure 5.49 shows a sample of all six heading levels and alignment possibilities in a BBEdit document, and **Figure 5.50** shows how the document appears in a Web browser.

Figure 5.50 The same document seen through Internet Explorer.

HEADING

Java Applet

The HTML Java Applet tool (see **Figure 5.51**) is similar to the HTML Form tool in that it assists you in linking to an applet rather than programming the applet.

To insert a Java Applet:

1. Open a document that will reference the applet.

2. Choose Applet from the HTML Java Applet submenu (see **Figure 5.52**) and complete the fields.

3. Choose the Param option and enter any parameters and values, if necessary (see **Figure 5.53**).

You can also use the Textflow option to insert the <TEXTFLOW></TEXTFLOW> tags to control how text appears on screen.

Figure 5.51 The HTML Java Applet tool menu.

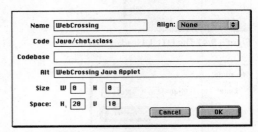

Figure 5.52 Use the Applet menu to identify your Applet, its code, and codebase, as well as placement options.

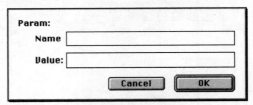

Figure 5.53 If necessary, choose the Param option to configure any parameters required to reference an applet.

Figure 5.54 The HTML Links tool menu.

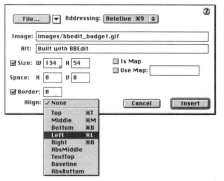

Figure 5.55 The Anchor tool is very comprehensive and includes all the options you need to create an anchor to any type of hyperlink.

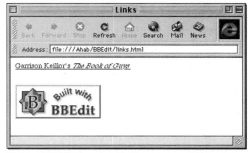

Figure 5.56 Use the Image menu to insert an inline image.

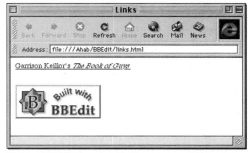

Figure 5.57 Anchors and links are easy to create using the HTML Links tool.

Links

The HTML Links tool (see **Figure 5.54**) allows you to create link anchors and insert images, including image maps. You'll use these two options frequently as you work with HTML documents, and the authors of the HTML Tools have done a great job to make these tasks as easy as possible.

To create an anchor for a hyperlink:

1. Position the cursor where you want the link will go.

2. Choose Anchor from the HTML Links submenu (see **Figure 5.55**) and complete the fields.

3. Enter the appropriate information about the link, including scheme (type), addressing, and the hyperlink reference. (All fields may not require information, however.)

4. Click the Insert button.

✔ Tips

■ Choose the File button to locate the hyperlink reference (HREF) document if it resides on your hard drive.

■ Use the Addressing option to have BBEdit automatically fill in the path as defined in your Preferences.

To insert an image:

1. Insert the cursor where the image will go.

2. Choose Image from the HTML Links submenu (see **Figure 5.56**) and complete the fields.

3. Enter the appropriate information about the image, including any alternative text, size information, alignment options, and whether it is an image map.

4. Click the Insert button.

Figure 5.57 shows how these two examples appear in a Web browser.

Lists

HTML 3.2 supports many different types of lists, which you can create using the HTML Lists tool (see **Figure 5.58**). Each type of list has slightly different attributes, but they are all created in much the same way. The following commands can be used to create a new list, or convert selected text into a list.

To create a list:

1. Insert the cursor where the list is to appear, or select some text to be converted into a list.

2. Choose the type of list from the HTML Lists submenu, or choose Options and select the type of list you'd like to create from the drop-down menu of list types.

3. Make any additional selections and press the Insert button.

For example, **Figure 5.59** shows the differences in the options when creating an unordered and an ordered list, and **Figure 5.60** shows how these lists appear in a Web browser.

To insert an item into an existing list:

1. Select the point at which the item is to be inserted.

2. Choose New Item from the HTML Lists submenu, and BBEdit will insert the <LI> tag.

Figure 5.58 The HTML Lists tool menu.

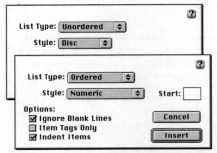

Figure 5.59 Different types of lists have different configuration attributes as well.

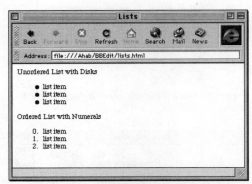

Figure 5.60 Two kinds of lists, an unordered list (top) and an ordered list (bottom).

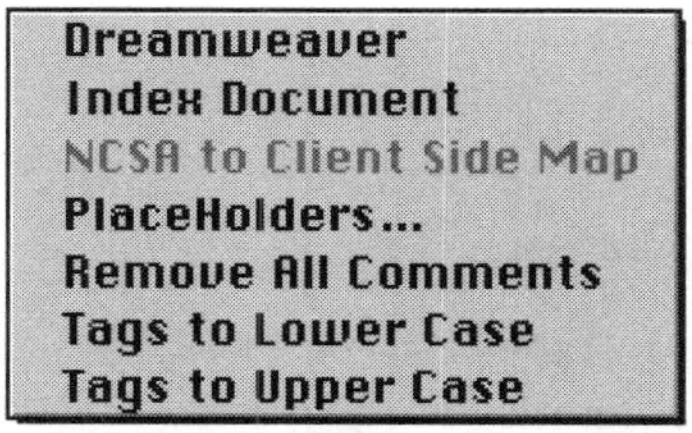

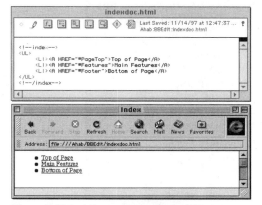

Figure 5.61 The HTML Misc(ellaneous) tool menu.

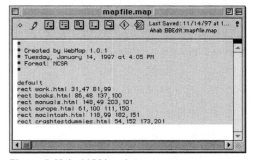

Figure 5.62 An index created using the Index Document tool.

Figure 5.63 An NCSA-style image map.

Figure 5.64 The same image map after being converted into a client-side image map.

Misc

The HTML Misc menu (see **Figure 5.61**) is home to several miscellaneous tools. Some of these tools appear in the HTML Tools palette under the Utilities button, and others appear as buttons unto themselves.

To invoke the Dreamweaver application:

1. Choose the Dreamweaver menu option to launch Dreamweaver, if installed on your computer.

To create an index of a document:

1. Choose the Index Document menu option to create an index of anchors that use the <A NAME= " > tag, which is placed at the top of your document. (see **Figure 5.62**).

To convert an NCSA image map file to a client-side image map:

1. Open an NCSA image map file.

2. Select the data to be converted (see **Figure 5.63**).

3. Choose the NCSA to Client Side Map option from the HTML Misc submenu and give the map a name (see **Figure 5.64**).

Misc

To insert a placeholder:

1. Move the cursor where the placeholder will go.

2. Choose PlaceHolders from the HTML Misc submenu (see **Figure 5.65**) and select a placeholder to insert.

We'll look at placeholders in detail in the next chapter.

To remove comments from a document:

1. Choose Remove All Comments from the HTML Misc submenu to remove any data contained between the <!-- --> tag, as well as the tag itself.

To convert tag case:

1. Choose Tags to Lower Case from the HTML Misc submenu to convert all tags (but not URLs and other possibly case sensitive data) to lower case.

2. Choose Tags to Upper Case from the HTML Misc submenu to similarly convert all tags to upper case.

✔ Tip

■ Remember that tags are not case sensitive, but some URLs are, especially on Unix-based Web servers.

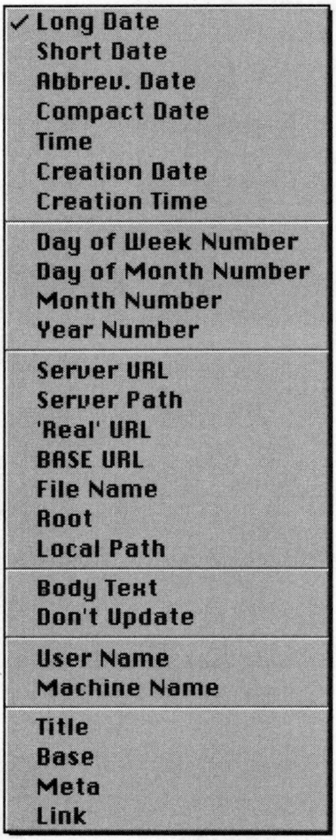

✓ Long Date
Short Date
Abbrev. Date
Compact Date
Time
Creation Date
Creation Time

Day of Week Number
Day of Month Number
Month Number
Year Number

Server URL
Server Path
'Real' URL
BASE URL
File Name
Root
Local Path

Body Text
Don't Update

User Name
Machine Name

Title
Base
Meta
Link

Figure 5.65 The PlaceHolders menu items.

Misc

Figure 5.66 The HTML Preview tool menu.

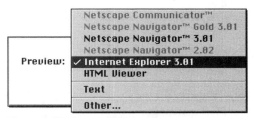

Figure 5.67 Choose a Web browser to serve as a default for previewing HTML documents.

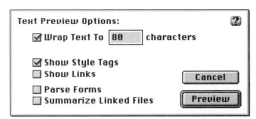

Figure 5.68 You can use BBEdit's built-in text viewer to preview Web pages.

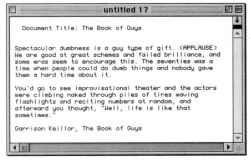

Figure 5.69 A Web page as seen in BBEdit's text viewer.

Preview

Since BBEdit is a text-based HTML editor, it relies on your using a Web browser to view the result your work. The HTML Preview tool (see **Figure 5.66**) may be configured to work with multiple Web browsers, as well as BBEdit's built-in text browsing capability.

To preview an HTML document:

1. Open an HTML document.

2. Choose Options from the HTML Preview submenu and select a Web browser (see **Figure 5.67**).

3. If you've already chosen a default Web browser for previewing, choose Preview from the HTML Preview submenu instead.

BBEdit will already know about most Web browsers you may have installed on your hard drive. You can select one of these or BBEdit's text browser (the Text option), or you can identify another Web browser by choosing Other.

If you choose BBEdit's text browser, you'll need to fill in a few configuration options first (see **Figure 5.68**) before it converts your document into a viewable Web page (see **Figure 5.69**).

PREVIEW

Styles

There are many text formatting styles in the HTML Styles tool (see **Figure 5.70**), and you'll probably use most of them before long. Keep in mind, however, that not all Web browsers support all text styles. If you include an unsupported style, the viewing browser will either ignore the styled text or display it as normal text.

To apply a style:

1. Open an HTML document and select some text to which a style will be applied.

2. Choose a style from the HTML Styles submenu or select **Options**, which opens the window shown in **Figure 5.71**, and select a style.

3. You can choose a style prior to highlighting text in your document and the style tag will be inserted by itself.

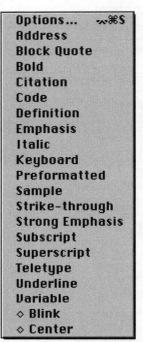

Figure 5.70 The HTML Styles tool menu.

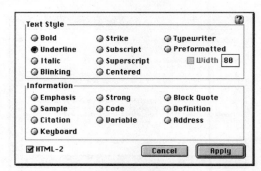

Figure 5.71 The Options portion of the HTML Styles tool menu.

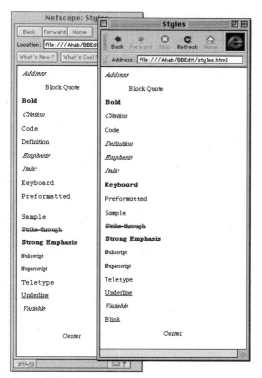

Figure 5.72 All but two styles (keyboard and blink) are supported equally by these two Web browsers.

Examples of the styles supported by the HTML Styles tool are shown in **Figure 5.72** as they appear in two Web browsers, Netscape Navigator 3 and Microsoft Internet Explorer 3.

<ADDRESS>Address</ADDRESS>
<BLOCKQUOTE>Block Quote</BLOCKQUOTE>
<B>Bold</B>
<CITE>Citation</CITE>
<CODE>Code</CODE>
<DFN>Definition</DFN>
<EM>Emphasis</EM>
<I>Italic</I>
<KBD>Keyboard</KBD>
<PRE>Preformatted</PRE>
<SAMP>Sample</SAMP>
<S>Strike-through</S>
<STRONG>Strong Emphasis</STRONG>
_{Subscript}
^{Superscript}
<TT>Teletype</TT>
<U>Underline</U>
<VAR>Variable</VAR>
<BLINK>Blink</BLINK>
<CENTER>Center</CENTER>

Stylesheets

Stylesheets, one of the latest features of HTML, is supported only by the most recent versions of Navigator and Internet Explorer. Stylesheets come in two flavors—Cascading Style Sheets (CSS) and JavaScript Style Sheets (JSS)—both of which may be used to store preferences about style formatting, such as font size and color.

BBEdit's HTML StyleSheet tool (see **Figure 5.73**) provides limited support for either variety of style sheets. With the HTML StyleSheet tool, you can insert a header and a blank <STYLE></STYLE> tag, but not the styles themselves.

To define a style sheet:

1. Open an HTML document and insert the cursor where the style sheet information will be located.

2. Choose Options from the HTML StyleSheet submenu (see **Figure 5.74**).

3. Enter the type of style sheet you are defining. The default is CSS1.

4. Whenever you choose the Style option from the HTML StyleSheet submenu, the same style sheet will be entered until you change the values under the Options menu again.

For example, the following CSS data will change any text in the <H1></H1> tag into bold and centered text with a level 1 heading (see **Figure 5.75**):

```
<STYLE TYPE="CSS1">
<!--
H1 {font style: italic}
H1 {text-align: center}
-->
</STYLE>
```

Figure 5.73 The HTML StyleSheet menu.

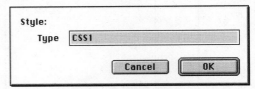

Figure 5.74 Define the type of style sheet using the StyleSheet Options menu.

Figure 5.75 A Web page that incorporates a Cascading Style Sheet.

Figure 5.76 The HTML Table tool menu.

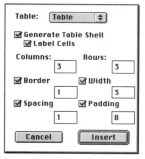

Figure 5.77 Use the Options menu choice to configure all your table variables.

Row_1_Col_1_	Row_1_Col_2_	Row_1_Col_3_
Row_2_Col_1_	Row_2_Col_2_	Row_2_Col_3_
Row_3_Col_1_	Row_3_Col_2_	Row_3_Col_3_

Figure 5.78 A sample table created using the Generate Table Shell option.

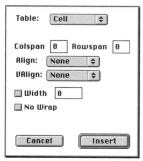

Figure 5.79 Choose any of the table options, or choose the Options menu and select an element to insert, such as a cell.

Table

The HTML Table tool (see **Figure 5.76**) has largely been replaced by the Table Builder application (discussed in detail in Chapter 7). However, you can still use the HTML Table tool to create tables, as well as convert delimited text into tables.

To create a table:

1. Open a document and place the cursor where you'd like to insert a table.

2. Select the HTML Table menu option to insert a table with its default values, or choose Options to open the window shown in **Figure 5.77**.

The result of accepting the default values is shown in **Figure 5.78**.

To edit a table:

1. Open a document containing a table and place the cursor where you'd like to insert a tag.

2. Select the tag from the HTML Table submenu, or choose Options and configure the appropriate tag from the pull-down menu (see **Figure 5.79**).

TABLE

91

To convert text into a table:

1. Open a document containing tab- or comma-delimited data and highlight it (see **Figure 5.80**).

2. Select Convert to Table from the HTML Table submenu.

3. Go to the Table pull-down menu and make sure the Generate Table Shell option is unchecked (see **Figure 5.77** above).

4. Go to the Convert option under the HTML Table pull-down menu and click the Convert button (see **Figure 5.81**), the result of which is shown in **Figure 5.82**.

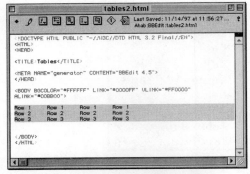

Figure 5.80 You can use the HTML Table tool to convert tab-delimited text like this into a table.

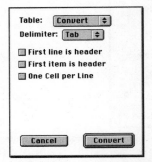

Figure 5.81 The Convert to Table options window.

Row 1	Row 1	Row 1	Row 1
Row 2	Row 2	Row 2	Row 2
Row 3	Row 3	Row 3	Row 3

Figure 5.82 Tab-delimited text converted into a table.

TABLE

| Comment |
| Uncomment |
| Entities... ⌥⌘E |
| Insert Hotlist... |
| PageMill Cleaner |
| Remove Tags |
| Translate... ⌥⌘T |
| Web Color Palette |

Figure 5.83 The HTML Utilities menu.

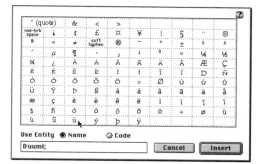

Figure 5.84 The Entities menu make inserting a character entity very easy.

Utilities

The final section of HTML Tools, HTML Utilities, is a collection of utilities designed to help users perform miscellaneous tasks associated with HTML authorship. The Utilities menu is shown in **Figure 5.83**.

To enter a comment:

1. Select Comment from the HTML Utilities submenu.

2. Go to the <!-- --> tag entered in your document and type in your comment.

To remove comments:

1. Select the text containing the comments to be removed, or select Command+A to select the contents of the entire document.

2. Select Uncomment from the HTML Utilities submenu.

To insert a character entity:

1. Position the cursor in your document where the entity is to be placed.

2. Select Entities from the HTML Utilities submenu.

3. Select an entity with the mouse and specify whether it should be entered as a name or code (see **Figure 5.84**).

4. Select the Insert button to insert the entity in your document.

To insert a hotlist:

1. Position the cursor in your document where the hotlist of bookmarks is to be inserted.

2. Select Insert Hotlist from the HTML Utilities submenu.

3. Choose either HTML Anchors, to create a set of hyperlinks, or Text List, to create a textual list of bookmarks, from the window shown in **Figure 5.85**.

Figure 5.86 shows what the HTML Anchors option looks like in Internet Explorer.

To clean up a document created using Adobe PageMill:

1. Open a document created by Adobe PageMill.

2. Select part or all of the text in the document.

3. Select PageMill Cleaner from the HTML Utilities submenu.

Gratuitous <BR>, <NATURALSIZE>, and other tags will be removed.

Figure 5.85 You can import a hotlist as hyperlinks or as plain text.

Figure 5.86 A sample of a hotlist of bookmarks imported as hyperlinks (HTML anchors).

Figure 5.87 An HTML document converted to text.

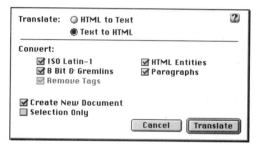

Figure 5.88 There are many translation options to choose from.

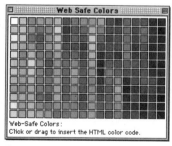

Figure 5.89 The Web Safe Colors palette makes inserting browser-safe colors as easy as possible.

To remove HTML tags from a document:

1. Open an HTML document created by BBEdit or any other HTML editor.

2. Select part or all of the text in the document.

3. Select Remove Tags from the HTML Utilities submenu.

Figure 5.87 contains the same document shown in Figure 5.86 after all its tags have been removed.

To translate a text document to HTML and vice versa:

1. Open a text or HTML document.

2. Select part or all of the text in the document.

3. Select Translate from the Utilities submenu (see Figure 5.88).

4. Choose whether you want to translate HTML to text, or text to HTML, and any additional options, then click the Translate button.

To insert a Web-safe color:

1. Insert the cursor in your document where the color reference is to be placed.

2. Select Web Color Palette from the Utilities submenu (see Figure 5.89).

3. Drag or click a color to insert it into your document.

TEMPLATES, PLACEHOLDERS, AND INCLUDES

Most Web sites consist of documents that have a similar structure or contain the same elements, such as headers and footers. Creating and maintaining these documents can be repetitive because you either have to type these same elements over and over, or cut and paste them from one document into another. Some large-scale Web sites use programs that automatically generate a whole new set of documents every time a header or footer is changed, but this beyond most Webmasters.

BBEdit has several solutions for this problem. You've seen how macros work in the previous chapter, and in Chapter 10 you'll see how to script BBEdit to perform repetitive tasks. In this chapter, we'll look at how to use HTML templates to save you time and effort in creating and maintaining groups of similar HTML documents, as well as how to use placeholders and file includes.

HTML templates are documents that contain predefined data, such as headers and footers; special phrases called *placeholders* that serve as shorthand for things like the current time and date; and special phrases called *file includes* (or just *includes*) that serve as placeholders for entire files. In fact, every time you create a new HTML document you are using BBEdit's default template, which automatically inserts several HTML tags and saves you the trouble of having to type them yourself.

Configuring Your Preferences

BBEdit installs several example templates in a folder called HTML Templates, which is located in the BBEdit root folder (see **Figure 6.1**). You can create one or more additional folders for different groups of templates, but you'll need to tell BBEdit where the folder is located.

To set the location of the HTML Templates folder:

1. Launch BBEdit and select Edit | Preferences (or press Command+;).

2. Select the HTML section of the Preferences (see **Figure 6.2**).

3. Identify a folder for your templates by either clicking the Set button or by dragging and dropping the folder onto the rectangular area to the left of the button (see **Figure 6.3**).

4. Click the Save button and your change will take effect immediately.

✔ Tips

■ You may want to maintain multiple template folders if you work on large projects and want to group your templates in separate folders.

■ It is possible to write an AppleScript to change the location of the HTML templates folder on the fly.

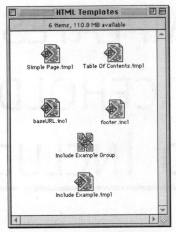

Figure 6.1 The HTML Templates root folder.

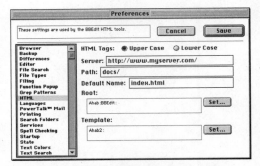

Figure 6.2 Configure the location of your HTML templates in the HTML section of BBEdit's Preferences.

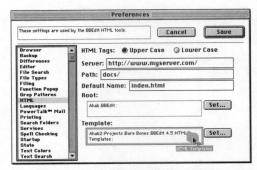

Figure 6.3 You can select the location of the HTML Templates folder by choosing the Set button, or by dragging and dropping the folder onto the Template area in the HTML Preferences.

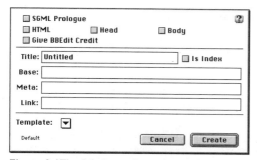

Figure 6.4 The default template isn't really a template, but it works the same way as your custom templates.

Choosing a Template

You have three main options when it comes to selecting an HTML template whenever you create a new HTML document:

- Use BBEdit's default template.

- Select the same template automatically whenever you create a new HTML document.

- Select a different template whenever you create a new HTML document.

If you choose File | New | Text Document (or Command+N) instead of choosing to create an HTML document, no template will be loaded and you'll be presented with a completely blank document.

To load the default template:

When you create a new HTML document by choosing File | New | HTML Document or by selecting the New Document button from the HTML Tools palette, the default template is automatically loaded. It's not actually a template in the same sense as a file called default.tmpl, but it serves the same purpose.

1. Create a new HTML document.

2. Look in the lower left-hand corner of the new document dialog box for the section entitled Template (see **Figure 6.4**)

3. The name of the template (Default) appears below.

4. Click the Create button to proceed.

To load another template:

You can select another template whenever you create a new HTML document:

1. Create a new HTML document.

2. Look in the lower left-hand corner of the new document dialog box for the section entitled Template.

3. Click on the drop-down triangle to reveal the contents of the Templates folder (specified in the Preferences).

4. Choose any entry other than Default (see **Figure 6.5**).

5. Click the **Create** button to proceed.

To load the same template again:

1. Create a new HTML document.

2. The same template will be loaded and appear as the default choice (see **Figure 6.6**)

3. Click the **Create** button to proceed.

✔ Tips

■ BBEdit remembers the last template used and will mark it as the default template until you change it.

■ BBEdit remembers the last template used even after you quit and restart BBEdit.

■ BBEdit will only look for templates in the same folder as the one specified in the Preferences. It will not allow you to look in subfolders relative to the template folder.

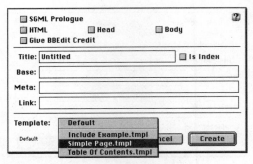

Figure 6.5 Choosing one of the three sample templates included with BBEdit.

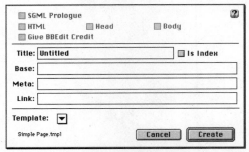

Figure 6.6 Look in the lower left-hand corner of the New Document dialog window to see which template you've selected.

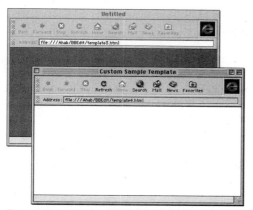

Figure 6.7 HTML documents created using the default template (background) and a custom template (foreground).

Figure 6.8 My custom template includes different colors for the background and links.

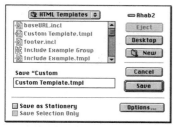

Figure 6.9 Be sure to save your templates in the HTML Templates folder with the extension .tmpl.

Figure 6.10 Choose a template when you create a new HTML document.

Working with Templates

Templates are text and HTML documents that end with the file extension .tmpl and are located in the designated HTML Templates folder. You can use any of the sample templates that come with BBEdit, or you can simply create a blank HTML document, customize it with your desired preferences, and then save it as your new default template. For example, I prefer all my document to have several custom <BODY> attributes, including a white background, so I created a template with these attributes and use it in place of BBEdit's default template, both of which are shown in **Figure 6.7**.

To create your own custom template:

1. Create an HTML document and customize it to your liking (see **Figure 6.8**).

2. Choose File | Save As and place it in your HTML Templates folder (see **Figure 6.9**).

3. To use the template, choose File | New | HTML Document and select your template from the **Template** selection area (see **Figure 6.10**).

Once your template is loaded, you can work with your new document as you would any other HTML document.

✔ Tips

■ If you choose any template other than the Default template, the checkboxes in the New HTML Document dialog box may be unavailable.

■ Creating a new document using a template will not erase or alter the template itself.

To use a basic template:

1. Choose File | New | HTML Document and select Table of Contents.tmpl from the Template selection area (see **Figure 6.11**).

2. Select the Create button, and the document will appear in a new window (see **Figure 6.12**).

3. Edit and save the document.

For example, **Figure 6.13** shows the result of creating a document using the Table of Contents.tmpl template. This example shows how you can use anchors to create a table of contents for easier navigation of potentially long documents, as well as how using a template can save you from having to type frequently used code over and over again.

This example template comprises mostly HTML code, but it also uses one command called a *placeholder* that takes the contents of the Title area of the New Document window and inserts it into the newly created HTML document.

The placeholder command looks like this in the template:

```
<TITLE>#TITLE#</TITLE>
```

So, whatever you type in the Title area will be inserted automatically in the HTML document, which appears in the title bar of the browser window. Let's look more closely at how templates can use placeholders before we look at placeholders in detail.

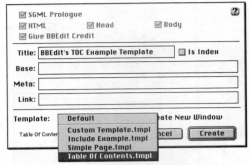

Figure 6.11 One of the sample templates provided as part of BBEdit.

Figure 6.12 The information highlighted here was automatically inserted by the template using a placeholder.

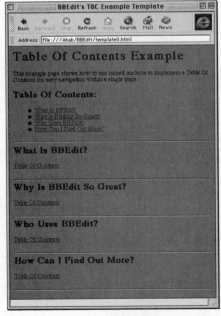

Figure 6.13 A document created using a template.

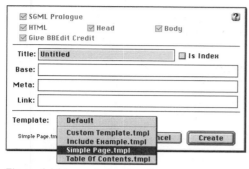

Figure 6.14 A sample template that uses numerous placeholders.

Figure 6.15 The HTML code generated by the template.

Figure 6.16 The code as viewed through a Web browser.

To use a sample placeholder in a template:

1. Choose File | New | HTML Document and select Sample Page.tmpl from the Template selection area (see **Figure 6.14**).

2. Select the Create button, and the document will appear in a new window (see **Figure 6.15**).

3. Save the document, and view the results in a Web browser (see **Figure 6.16**).

4. Even though this example template is named Sample Page.tmpl, it is really more advanced than the previous example because it shows how placeholders can be used to perform several tasks, including automatically entering your name, the date, and your e-mail address. The placeholders used here look like this in the template:

   <TITLE>#USERNAME#'s First Page</TITLE>

   <H1>#USERNAME#'s First Page</H1>

   Created by <PERSON>#USERNAME#</PERSON> on #LONGDATE#.

   For more information, please <A HREF="mailto:#IC_EMAIL#"> send mail to #IC_EMAIL#</A>.

Placeholders aren't part of templates per se, but they can be used very effectively in conjunction with templates to save you even more time in creating HTML documents.

WORKING WITH TEMPLATES

Placeholders

Placeholders work like shorthand in that they are abbreviations for longer words of phrases. They can be used in templates or anywhere in a BBEdit document, but when they're used in templates there is no need to convert them into their nonabbreviated form using the Update command. However, if you manually insert a placeholder in a document, you'll have to perform this operation to convert the placeholders.

Using a placeholder in an HTML document:

1. Create a new HTML document.

2. Insert a placeholder such as #LONGDATE# into the document (see **Figure 6.17**).

3. Choose Update Current Document from the Tools | HTML Document | Update menu (see **Figure 6.18**).

4. BBEdit will convert the placeholder (see **Figure 6.19**).

✔ Tips

- Placeholders can be used in any type of BBEdit document.

- When used in a template, placeholders are automatically updated.

- You'll have to manually update placeholders when using them in any document not created by a template.

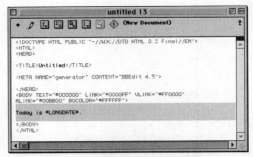

Figure 6.17 A placeholder manually entered into an HTML document.

Figure 6.18 You can choose to update either the current document or all the documents in your document root folder.

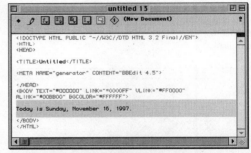

Figure 6.19 The same placeholders after updating.

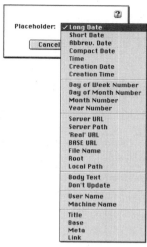

Figure 6.20 The Placeholders tool options.

Table 6.1 lists the placeholders that are available in the version of HTML Tools included in BBEdit 4.5.1. Most, but not all, of these placeholders are also available through the Tools | HTML Tools | Misc | Placeholders menu, shown in **Figure 6.20**.

BBEdit provides yet another way to easily insert repetitive information into documents, either manually or via templates, through the use of file includes.

Table 6.1

Placeholders and Their Values

PLACEHOLDER	VALUE	PLACEHOLDER	VALUE
#ABBREVDATE#	The current date, abbreviated	#META#	The META tag as defined in the Meta field of the New Document tool
#BASE#	The BASE tag as defined in the Base field in the New Document tool	#MODIFIEDDATE#	The date the document is updated using the Update tool
#BASE_URL#	The BASE URL as specified in the current document	#MODIFIEDTIME#	The time the document is updated using the Update tool
#BODYTEXT#	The current contents of the window (if any) will be placed in the position specified in your HTML Preferences	#MONTHLYDAYNUM#	Day of the month, expressed numerically
		#MONTHNUM#	The month, expressed numerically
#COMPDATE#	The current date, compacted	#PATH#	The path to the document as specified in the HTML section of the Preferences
#CREATIONDATE#	The creation date of the working document		
#CREATIONTIME#	The creation time of the working document	#REAL_URL#	The URL for the current document.
#DONT_UPDATE#	Tells the Update tool to ignore a document during processing	#ROOT#	The path to the root directory as specified in the HTML section of the Preferences
#FILENAME#	The filename of the working document	#ROOTPATH#	The path from the "server root" to the current document
#IC_EMAIL#	The e-mail address contained in Internet Config	#SERVER#	The URL of your Web server as specified in the HTML section of the Preferences
#IC_ORGANIZATION#	The organization identified in Internet Config	#SHORTDATE#	The current date, in short format
#IC_REALNAME#	The real name value identified in Internet Config	#TIME#	The time the document was created using a template or is updated using the Update tool
#LINK#	The value in the Link field in the New Document tool	#TITLE#	The title of the document as defined in the Title field in the New Document tool
#LOCALPATH#	The path to the local working document	#USERNAME#	Your user name as defined in File Sharing
#LONGDATE#	The current date, in long format	#WEEKNUM#	The current week, expressed numerically
#MACHINE#	The name of your Mac as defined for File Sharing	#YEARNUM#	The current year, expressed numerically

Includes

File includes, or just *includes*, work just like placeholders except instead of inserting small pieces of data wherever a placeholder is found, they insert the contents of whole files. Includes are best used to insert repetitive sections of HTML documents such as headers and footers, as well as lists and navigational menus. Using includes in BBEdit is another trick of the software programming trade that carried over into HTML. Programmers often use the same chunk of code over and over again, and the creators of BBEdit quickly saw that HTML authors work in much the same way.

Includes are inserted into a document like this:

#include "filename.html

Like placeholders, includes must also reside in your HTML Templates folder, but they do not require a special filename extension.

Figure 6.21 An example of an include file.

Figure 6.22 The include command inserted in an HTML document.

Figure 6.23 The Update tool works on includes as well as placeholders.

Figure 6.24 An HTML document after an include has been inserted.

To use an include:

1. Create a document to serve as an include file, such as footer.html (see **Figure 6.21**), and place it in the HTML Templates folder.

2. Create a new HTML document.

3. Insert an include such as #include "footer.html" into the document (see **Figure 6.22**).

4. Choose Update Current Document from the Tools | HTML Document | Update menu (see **Figure 6.23**).

5. BBEdit will insert the include (see **Figure 6.24**).

✔ Tips

- Includes can be used in any type of BBEdit document.

- Includes, like placeholders, are automatically updated (inserted) when used in a template.

- You'll have to manually update (insert) the includes when using them in any document not created by a template.

When a document is updated, the reference to the include is overwritten by the contents of the include file. You can use a persistent include to prevent this from happening. A persistent include is embedded in an opening and terminating comment as follows:

```
<!-- #include "footer.html" -->
<!-- end include -->
```

Both of these comments will remain after the document has been updated.

To use a persistent include:

1. Create a document to serve as an include file and place it in the HTML Templates folder.

2. Create a new HTML document.

3. Insert an include within a comment such as `<!-- #include "footer.html" -->` and terminate it using `<!-- end include -->` (see **Figure 6.25**).

4. Choose Update Current Document from the Tools | HTML Document | Update menu (see **Figure 6.26**).

5. BBEdit will insert the persistent include without removing the include command from the document (see **Figure 6.27**).

Figure 6.25 The persistent include command inserted in an HTML document.

Figure 6.26 The Update tool works on persistent includes as well as includes and placeholders.

Figure 6.27 An HTML document after a persistent include has been inserted.

TABLE BUILDER

BBEdit Table Builder is a recent addition to BBEdit that allows you to create complex tables using a graphical interface. Of course, you can still use the Table tool to create and edit tables, but Table Builder is far more powerful and easier to use.

Unlike the Table tool, Table Builder is a separate application that hooks into BBEdit, allowing you to export tables into BBEdit after you've created and edited them to your liking. Likewise, BBEdit allows you to export tables into Table Builder, so the two work hand-in-hand and take advantage of the other's strengths.

Table Builder isn't nearly as complex an application as BBEdit, but it is as good a table editor as BBEdit is a text editor. Because it's such a focused application, using Table Builder is very intuitive.

Configuring Table Builder

Table Builder is installed along with the
BBEdit application (see **Figure 7.1**) and isn't
included as a separate item in the Custom
Installation section of the installation process.
Since Table Builder is dedicated to such a nar-
rowly defined task, it doesn't require a lot of
your system resources to operate. It defaults
to using the following system resources:

- 1MB of RAM
- 150K of disk space

As with BBEdit, if you plan to edit very large
tables you may want to go ahead and give it
more memory.

To give Table Builder additional memory:

1. Select the Table Builder application icon
and choose File | Get Info (or Command+I),
as in **Figure 7.2**.

2. Increase the amount of RAM in the
Preferred Size box. In my case, I doubled
it to 2MB.

3. Close the Get Info dialog box.

Table Builder has no Preferences to configure,
so once you've completed the above step
(if it's necessary in your case), you're done.

CONFIGURING TABLE BUILDER

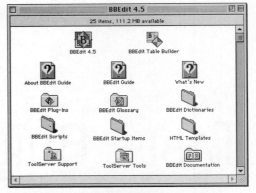

Figure 7.1 Table Builder is installed as part of the
BBEdit application and is not optional.

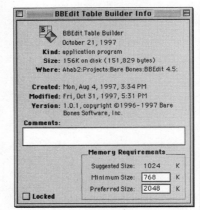

Figure 7.2 Increase the amount of RAM dedicated to
Table Builder if you plan to work with large tables.

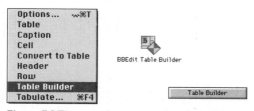

Figure 7.3 There are three ways to launch the Table Builder application.

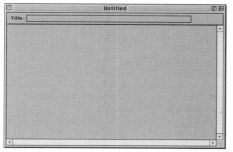

Figure 7.4 Table Builder first creates a blank HTML document before you can add a new table.

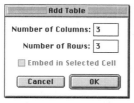

Figure 7.5 When you add a new table to a Table Builder document, you'll need to tell Table Builder a little bit about the structure of the table.

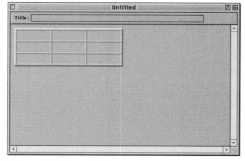

Figure 7.6 A new table.

Creating and Editing Tables

The best way to get started with Table Builder is to create a table from scratch, and then learn how to import and export tables to and from BBEdit.

To create a table:

1. Launch Table Builder by double-clicking the Table Builder application icon, by selecting Table Builder from the HTML Tools palette, or by selecting Tools | HTML Table | Table Builder (see **Figure 7.3**).

2. Select File | New (or Command+N) to open a new document (see **Figure 7.4**).

3. Choose Table | Add Table (or Command+E) to insert a new table in the blank document.

4. Specify in the Add Table dialog window how many columns and rows you want your table to have (see **Figure 7.5**) and click the OK button.

5. A new table will be inserted into the document (see **Figure 7.6**).

When you create a new document in Table Builder, you're actually creating an HTML document first, then inserting a table into that document. Although the resulting HTML document contains most of the same coding as a BBEdit document, it's not yet possible to use templates with Table Builder documents. They'll have all the default attributes of a basic HTML document, such as no background or link colors, and you can add additional tables (but no other HTML data) to the same document.

To place additional tables in a document:

1. Open a Table Builder document containing a table.

2. Choose Table | Add Table (or Command+E) to insert another table in the document, following the same steps as before to select the number or columns and rows.

3. An additional table will be inserted into the same document (see **Figure 7.7**).

✔ Tips

- Table Builder does more than import and export to BBEdit—it allows you to create and save entire documents.

- Table Builder can open some but not all documents containing tables created using applications other than Table Builder and BBEdit.

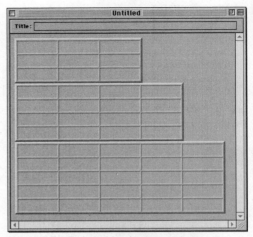

Figure 7.7 A Table Builder document can contain multiple tables, as in this example.

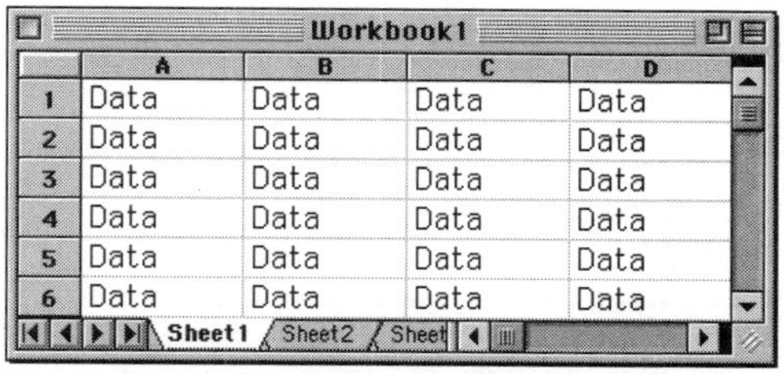

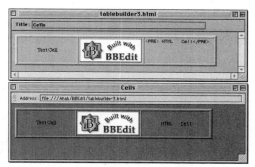

Figure 7.8 HTML tables are based on spreadsheets like this one, dividing the window into cells, rows, and columns.

Figure 7.9 Table Builder recognizes three types of cells: text, image, and HTML.

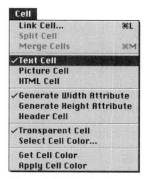

Figure 7.10 Click once to select a cell.

Figure 7.11 Use the Cell menu to tell Table Builder what type of cell you want.

Working with Tables

Unlike BBEdit, Table Builder is a graphical editing tool, meaning that you can use the cursor to drag and resize tables, and any changes you make show up in real time as they will appear in a Web browser. You can use the familiar editing capabilities of the Mac OS, including highlighting, copying, cutting, and pasting, but drag and drop support isn't available in this version of Table Builder

Tables consist of cells of data arranged in rows and columns, as in spreadsheet applications such as Microsoft Excel or Lotus 1-2-3 (see **Figure 7.8**). Table Builder is a bit different in that it distinguishes among three types of cell:

- Text Cell (for text)
- Picture Cell (for images)
- HTML Cell (for manually entered HTML formatting instructions).

This may seem a bit strange at first, but take a look at **Figure 7.9**, which shows a sample of each of these three types of cells in Table Builder (top) and a Web browser (bottom). Table Builder recognizes that tables often consist of different types of data and allows you to easily identify these types of data on a cell-by-cell basis.

To select a cell type:

1. Select a cell by clicking on it once (see **Figure 7.10**).

2. Select a cell type by choosing Cell | Text Cell, Cell|Picture Cell, or Code|HTML Cell, as in **Figure 7.11**.

You can also change the width and height of a cell by manually entering the numeric values (in pixels) for height and width, or by manually dragging the cell borders until you like what you see.

To resize a cell numerically:

1. Select a cell.

2. Choose Table | Row Height and Column Width and enter the new values (see **Figure 7.12**).

To resize a cell manually:

1. Select a cell.

2. Grab one side of the cell with the mouse and drag it up, down, left, or right (see **Figure 7.13**).

After you've resized your table, you should tell Table Builder to preserve these dimensions by adding commands to the HTML code it generates concerning the height and width of the cells.

Preserving cell dimensions:

1. Resize the table to suit your needs.

2. Go to the Cell menu and choose Generate Width Attribute and Generate Height Attribute (see **Figure 7.14**).

3. Save your document.

When Table Builder writes the table data to a file, it will include the height and width attributes in the appropriate table data <TD> tags. For example, the code generated for the newly resized cells in the above figure looks like this:

```
<TD WIDTH="151">
<TD HEIGHT="65">
```

Once you've done this you're ready to edit the cell.

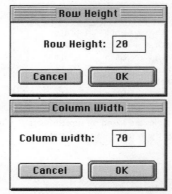

Figure 7.12 Use these commands to manually resize a cell.

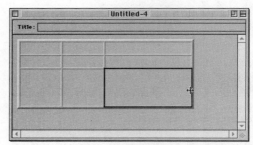

Figure 7.13 You can also drag any cell border to resize that cell.

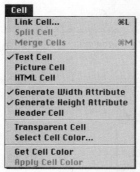

Figure 7.14 Make these selections to preserve your exact cell dimensions.

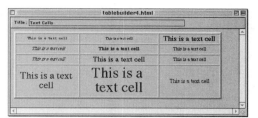

Figure 7.15 A table of text cells as seen in Table Builder.

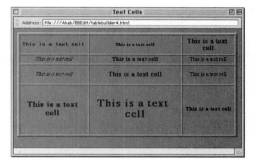

Figure 7.16 The text cells as seen in a Web browser.

Figure 7.17 Table Builder's Undo command isn't as powerful as BBEdit's, allowing only one Undo command at a time.

Figure 7.18 A table of HTML cells as seen in Table Builder.

Figure 7.19 The HTML cells as seen in a Web browser.

Editing Text Cells

There's a different way to edit each of the three cell types. Many of the actions are the same, but Table Builder gives you different options for each type of cell.

To edit a text cell:

1. Select a cell.

2. Identify it as a text cell.

3. Start typing in the cell, or copy and paste text into the cell (see **Figure 7.15**).

Figure 7.16 shows how the table looks in a Web browser.

✔ Tips

■ You can cut and paste into cells just as you would with any other HTML document using BBEdit.

■ Unlike BBEdit, the Undo command will reverse only your most recent action (using Edit | Undo, or Command+Z, as in **Figure 7.17**).

To edit an HTML cell:

1. Select a cell.

2. Identify it as a HTML cell.

3. Start typing in the cell, adding any HTML tags you'd like (see **Figure 7.18**).

Figure 7.19 shows how the table looks in a Web browser.

✔ Tip

■ You can use any HTML tag in a table that you'd normally use in any other HTML document.

EDITING TEXT CELLS

To edit an image cell:

1. Select a cell.

2. Identify it as an image cell. A small blank image icon will appear to let you know that it is indeed an image cell (see **Figure 7.20**).

3. Double-click the image icon in the image cell and use the Image Info dialog box to choose and configure you image file (see **Figure 7.21**).

4. Click the OK button and the image will be inserted into your Table Builder document (see **Figure 7.22**).

Figure 7.23 shows how the table looks in a Web browser.

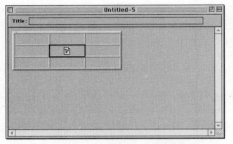

Figure 7.20 Image cells use icons like this one use to remind you that the cell is an image cell.

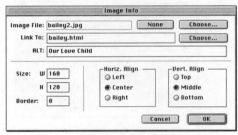

Figure 7.21 The Image Info configuration window, where you can easily locate and configure an image for inclusion in a table. Also, notice all the linking and alignment attributes for the image.

Figure 7.22 A table with an image cell in the center.

Figure 7.23 The same table as seen in a Web browser.

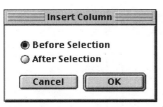

Figure 7.24 The Insert Column dialog box.

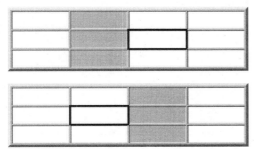

Figure 7.25 Two tables with newly inserted columns.

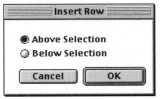

Figure 7.26 The Insert Row dialog box.

Figure 7.27 Two tables with newly inserted rows.

Adding and Removing Cells

After you have created and edited a table, you may find it necessary to go back and resize a table by adding or removing cells, rows, and columns. Table Builder allows you to not only add and delete entire rows and columns, but also to merge multiple cells into one, and divide (split) one cell into several.

To insert a column:

1. Select a cell in the column adjacent to where the new column will be added.

2. Choose Table | Insert Column (see **Figure 7.24**).

3. Choose whether to insert the new column before or after the currently selected column, then click the OK button.

Figure 7.25 shows two examples of inserting a column before the selection (top) and after the selection (bottom), with the new column in the darker shade.

To insert a row:

1. Select a cell in the row adjacent to where the new row will be added.

2. Choose Table | Insert Row (see **Figure 7.26**).

3. Choose whether to insert the new row above or below the currently selected row, then click the OK button.

For example, **Figure 7.27** shows two examples of inserting a row above the selection (top) and below the selection (bottom), with the new row in the darker shade.

To merge multiple cells into one:

1. Select the cells to be merged (see **Figure 7.28**).

2. Choose Cell | Merge Cells.

Figure 7.29 shows three cells that have been merged into a single cell.

To split one cell into multiple cells:

1. Select the cell to be split (see **Figure 7.30**).

2. Choose Cell | Split.

Figure 7.31 shows one large cell split into three smaller cells.

✔ Tips

- You must first select the cell or cells before the appropriate Merge or Split commands will be available in the Cell menu.

- Choose Command+Z to undo a merge or split.

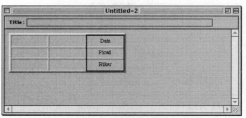

Figure 7.28 Three cells to be merged into one.

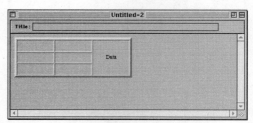

Figure 7.29 A table with merged cells.

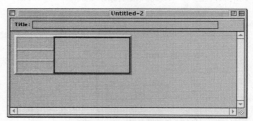

Figure 7.30 A large cell to be split into multiple cells.

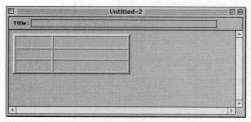

Figure 7.31 A table whose cells have been split.

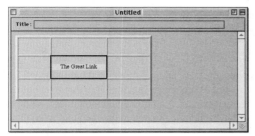

Figure 7.32 Linking text in a cell.

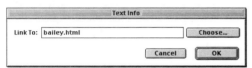

Figure 7.33 Linking data in a cell to a URL.

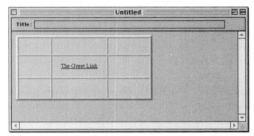

Figure 7.34 Table Builder displays hyperlinks just as they'll appear in a Web browser.

Linking Text

We've already seen how to insert an image and then link it to another document, now let's see how to do this with text. Table Builder doesn't provide all the bells and whistles that BBEdit does to help you create hyperlinks, but it will get the job done.

To link text in a cell:

1. Select a text cell.

2. Choose Cell | Link Cell (see **Figure 7.32**).

3. Enter the URL for the link, or select the Select button and locate the file manually (see **Figure 7.33**), then click the OK button.

4. The cell data will then become a hyperlink (see **Figure 7.34**).

LINKING TEXT

Importing and Exporting Tables

Table Builder and BBEdit work very well together to exchange table information between the two programs.

To import to Table Builder a table from another program:

1. Choose File | Import and select a document containing table data.

To export a table from Table Builder to BBEdit:

1. Open a document in BBEdit.

2. Place the cursor where the table is to be placed.

3. Open a table in Table Builder and choose File | Sent to BBEdit (or Command+Y), as in **Figure 7.35**.

The table (but none of the other HTML code) in Table Builder will then be placed in the BBEdit document (see **Figure 7.36**).

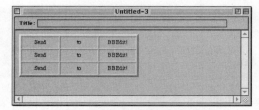

Figure 7.35 You can export any table from Table Builder into BBEdit.

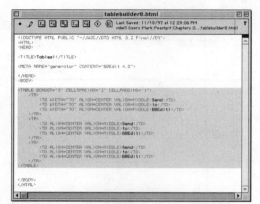

Figure 7.36 When a table is exported to BBEdit from Table Builder, only the <TABLE> </TABLE> data is exchanged.

UTILITIES & PLUG-INS

8

BBEdit uses several different approaches to extend its text manipulation and HTML authoring capabilities, including

- utilities and plug-ins
- Internet applications
- scripting

This chapter covers the utilities and plug-ins that are not addressed in Chapter 5, which is on the suite of plug-ins collectively known as HTML Tools. In later chapters, we'll talk about the helper applications that allow BBEdit to collaborate with Internet-based applications, and how to script BBEdit to perform routine tasks.

BBEdit uses certain utilities and plug-ins in the same way that Web browsers like Netscape Navigator and Microsoft Internet Explorer do. They provide features that, while not part of the BBEdit application itself, allow BBEdit users to perform tasks as though they were built into the application itself.

Plug-ins are especially useful because they provide BBEdit with new features without making you wait for the next revision of the application. This extensible approach is perfect for HTML authors because the ongoing browser wars between Netscape and Microsoft often result in changes in the way that HTML tags are implemented for use with a particular browser. Because BBEdit is extensible, software programmers can easily rewrite or create plug-ins to take advantage of these new HTML features.

About BBEdit Utilities

When you perform a standard or "easy" installation of BBEdit, several utilities are installed into a folder called BBEdit Utilities (see **Figure 8.1**).

- AppleMail Redirector
- Drop•BB
- SimpleText Redirector
- TextChanger 2.0

While these utilities perform a variety of functions relating to BBEdit, they are not integrated with BBEdit in any way unless you configure them to be. Therefore, you can elect to use them, or you can simply delete them and, if necessary, reinstall them at a later time.

(Re)Installing the BBEdit Utilities:

1. Insert the BBEdit installation CD-ROM.

2. Choose Custom Install.

3. Scroll down and select one or more of the BBEdit Utilities.

4. Quit the installation program.

Figure 8.2 shows the installation options to select when using your BBEdit installation CD-ROM to reinstall the BBEdit Utilities.

✔ Tip

- You do not need to restart your computer when installing just the BBEdit Utilities.

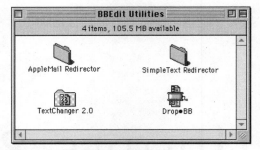

Figure 8.1 The BBEdit Utilities folder.

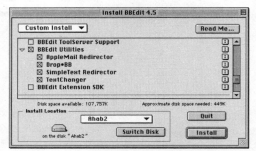

Figure 8.2 You can always reinstall the BBEdit Utilities from the BBEdit CD-ROM if you deleted them previously.

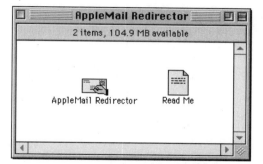

Figure 8.3 The AppleMail Redirector utility.

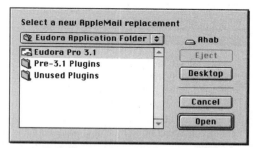

Figure 8.4 Choose an e-mail client to replace AppleMail.

AppleMail Redirector

The AppleMail Redirector utility, an application written by Pablo J. Fritz using AppleScript, takes mail intended for AppleMail and sends it to the e-mail client of your choice. Used in conjunction with BBEdit, this utility is particularly effective if you're using BBEdit and PowerTalk mail, but you can also use it to redirect mail to other e-mail applications, such as Eudora.

To install AppleMail Redirector

1. Remove AppleMail from your computer.

2. Launch AppleMail Redirector (see **Figure 8.3**) by double-clicking the application icon.

3. When prompted, select the e-mail client you'd like to use in place of AppleMail (see **Figure 8.4**).

✔ Tip

■ Leave the AppleMail Redirector open and allow it to run in the background for faster operation.

APPLEMAIL REDIRECTOR

Drop•BB

Drop•BB is a handy utility (see **Figure 8.5**) that converts any plain ASCII text file into a BBEdit file. BBEdit files are also ASCII text files, of course, but Drop•BB works by changing a file's creator code so that it becomes a BBEdit file. **Figure 8.6** shows a SimpleText file that will be converted to BBEdit using the following steps.

To convert a text file using Drop•BB:

1. Launch Drop•BB by double-clicking the application icon.

2. Choose File | Select File and locate a file to convert (see **Figure 8.7**).

3. The file is converted without any changes to the filename, which can then be opened in BBEdit by double-clicking on the file icon (see **Figure 8.8**).

✔ Tips

■ You can also launch Drop•BB by dropping any text file or folder of files onto the application icon.

■ Since the file is remains a text file after its conversion, you can still open it using the text editor that originally created it.

Figure 8.5 The Drop•BB utility.

Figure 8.6 A SimpleText file to be converted using Drop•BB.

Figure 8.7 Choose a file for conversion using the Select File window, or by dropping a file onto the Drop•BB icon.

Figure 8.8 A SimpleText file converted to a BBEdit file using Drop•BB.

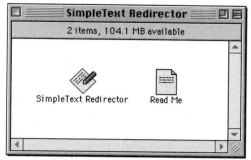

Figure 8.9 The SimpleText Redirector utility.

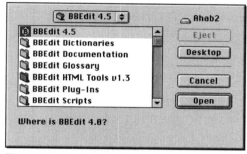

Figure 8.10 Choose BBEdit to replace SimpleText.

SimpleText Redirector

SimpleText Redirector is a utility based on the same principle (and AppleScript code) as AppleMail Redirector. But instead of redirecting e-mail requests, SimpleText Redirector takes requests for the SimpleText application and passes them on to BBEdit. So when you attempt to open a SimpleText document, it is opened by BBEdit instead.

This process differs from the way that Drop•BB is used to convert a document, in that Drop•BB requires manual intervention to convert files. SimpleText Redirector runs in the background and makes the conversion for you automatically.

To install SimpleText Redirector:

1. Remove all copies of SimpleText from your computer.

2. Launch SimpleText Redirector (see **Figure 8.9**) by double-clicking the application icon.

3. When prompted, select the e-mail client you'd like to use in place of AppleMail (see **Figure 8.10**).

✔ Tip

■ Leave the SimpleText Redirector open and allow it to run in the background for faster operation.

SIMPLETEXT REDIRECTOR

TextChanger

TextChanger is the most sophisticated of the three BBEdit Utilities. It's an application that performs the same purpose as Drop•BB but can also scan entire disks and zap the resource fork of text files so they can be used more reliably on non-Mac OS Web servers.

TextChanger can also run in the background and alert you when it encounters a new file type, at which time it will open a dialog box and present you with options relating to what to do with the file.

To scan a folder or disk and convert files to BBEdit:

1. Launch TextChanger (see **Figure 8.11**) by double-clicking the application icon.

2. Choose File | Scan Folder and locate folder or disk to scan for text files (see **Figure 8.12**).

3. TextChanger will start scanning. Each time it comes across a new file type, the window shown in **Figure 8.13** will appear.

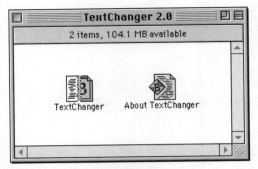

Figure 8.11 The TextChanger utility.

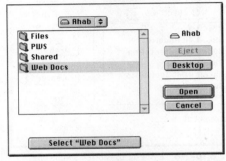

Figure 8.12 Choose a folder or disk to scan for text files.

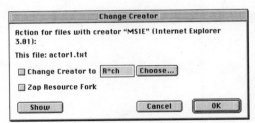

Figure 8.13 For every new file type TextChanger encounters, you'll need to make a few decisions as to what to do with these files in the future.

TEXTCHANGER

To change a file type to BBEdit:

For each new file type TextChanger encounters during a scan or as it runs in the background, you'll need to make the following decisions.

1. Select the **Change Creator to** checkbox to change the file's creator type to BBEdit.

2. Enter R*ch to convert the creator to BBEdit.

3. Click the **Choose** button and select an example file of the application to which the file type is to be converted, if not BBEdit/R*ch.

4. Check the **Zap Resource Fork** checkbox to delete the file's resource fork.

5. Click the Show button to reveal the document in the Finder.

6. Click the OK button to proceed with the scan and repeat this process every time a new file type is encountered.

✔ Tips

■ TextChanger will not convert or change any of the file types unless the **Change Creator to** checkbox is selected.

Plug-ins

We've seen the most popular BBEdit plug-ins earlier in the book, in the chapter on HTML Tools, but now we're going to look at some of the others that don't necessarily fit into a category of HTML tools or tasks.

The following plug-ins are accessible through the Tools menu (see **Figure 8.14**).

Add/Remove Line Numbers

The Add/Remove Line Numbers plug-in adds or removes line numbers not in the frame of a window, but in the a document itself (see **Figure 8.15**).

Columnize

The Columnize plug-in takes the selected data and rearranges it into user-defined columns (see **Figure 8.16**).

Compiler Tools

The Compiler Tools plug-in opens any compiler tools that you may have installed for easy access.

Concatenate

The Concatenate plug-in concatenates (adds) multiple documents together to form a single document (see **Figure 8.17**).

Convert To ASCII

The Convert To ASCII plug-in takes 8-bit text such as foreign languages and converts it into 7-bit (a.k.a. ASCII) text (see **Figure 8.18**).

Figure 8.14 The Tools menu.

Figure 8.15 The Add/Remove Line Numbers plug-in.

Figure 8.16 The Columnize plug-in.

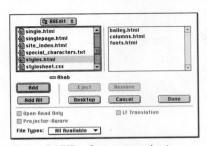

Figure 8.17 The Concatenate plug-in.

Figure 8.18 The Convert To ASCII plug-in.

PLUG-INS

Figure 8.19 The Copy Lines Containing plug-in.

Figure 8.20 The Cut Lines Containing plug-in.

Figure 8.21 The Educate Quotes plug-in.

Figure 8.22 The Embolden plug-in.

Figure 8.23 The FontSize+1 plug-in.

Figure 8.24 The FTP plug-in.

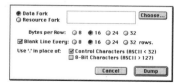

Figure 8.25 The Hex Dump plug-in.

Copy Lines Containing

The Copy Lines Containing plug-in looks at every line in a file and copies each line that contains the selected terms into the Clipboard (see **Figure 8.19**).

Cut Lines Containing

The opposite of the previous plug-in, the Cut Lines Containing plug-in looks at every line in a file and cuts each line containing the selected terms (see **Figure 8.20**).

Educate Quotes

The Educate Quotes plug-in exchanges all styles of quotation marks (straight, double, single) for curly quotes (see **Figure 8.21**)

Embolden

The Embolden plug-in takes the selected HTML data and encloses it in <B> </B> tags (see **Figure 8.22**).

Fix BinHex File

The Fix BinHex File plug-in makes corrections to improperly coded BinHex files.

FontSize+1

The FontSize+1 plug-in takes the selected HTML data and increases the relative font size by +1 (see **Figure 8.23**).

FTP

The FTP plug-in (which doesn't appear in the Tools menu) allows you to open, edit, and save documents on FTP servers through the File menu (see **Figure 8.24**). This is very useful when your HTML documents reside on Web servers that don't support AppleTalk.

Hex Dump

The Hex Dump plug-in is an obscure tool used by programmers to display the contents of a file's data fork in hexadecimal form (see **Figure 8.25**).

PLUG-INS

Internet Tools

The Internet Tools plug-in displays a floating palette that lists the helper applications assigned by the Internet Config application (see **Figure 8.26**).

Make Prototypes

The Make Prototypes plug-in is a programming tool that exports code into a prototype file.

Prefix/Suffix Lines

The Prefix/Suffix Lines plug-in allows you to add user-defined characters at the beginning or end of every line in a document (see **Figure 8.27**).

Project Statistics

The Project Statistics plug-in allows you to view important statistics about a project file for such programming environments as CodeWarrior and Symantec C.

Send PostScript

The Send PostScript plug-in provides a shortcut to send the current document as a PostScript file to a PostScript printer.

Sort

The Sort plug-in provides several sorting options that allow you to rearrange the contents of files (see **Figure 8.28**).

Un/Comment

The Un/Comment plug-in allows you to insert and remove comments in several types of programming languages, including HTML which uses **<!-- -->** to indicate comments (see **Figure 8.29**).

Figure 8.26 The Internet Tools plug-in.

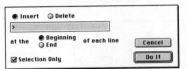

Figure 8.27 The Prefix/Suffix Lines plug-in.

Figure 8.28 The Sort plug-in.

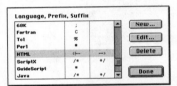

Figure 8.29 The Un/Comment plug-in.

9

INTERNET SERVICES

BBEdit is tightly integrated with just about any type of Internet-based application you can think of, due mostly to its use of the Internet Config application. But, as we've seen with the FTP plug-in, BBEdit is also capable of utilizing the Internet itself. Internet Config allows you to access Internet applications from within BBEdit, and to access BBEdit through these same Internet applications.

Installing Internet Config

Internet Config is installed along with BBEdit if you choose the Easy Install option. Many other applications also place a copy of Internet Config on your Mac's hard drive when they are installed, so you may have multiple copies on your hard drive. You should probably turn all of them off except the newest version.

To reinstall Internet Config:

1. Launch the BBEdit installation program on your BBEdit CD-ROM.

2. Choose Custom Install; scroll down to near the bottom of the screen and select Internet Config (see **Figure 9.1**), and click the Install button.

3. After the program has quit, the folder shown in **Figure 9.2** will be available on your hard drive.

Internet Config installs several files, but the following two are important to the successful operation of the program:

■ Internet Config Extension

■ Internet Config application

The Extension is located in the Extensions folder in your System Folder, and you'll never interact with it. The Internet Config application, on the other hand, is where you'll go to configure BBEdit and other Internet applications for use with each other. The rest of this chapter is concerned with this application.

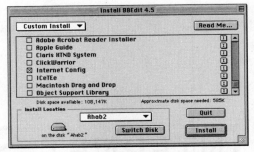

Figure 9.1 Reinstalling Internet Config Extension from the BBEdit CD-ROM.

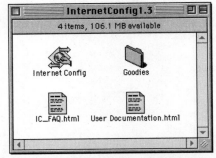

Figure 9.2 A typical installation of Internet Config on your computer's hard drive will look something like this.

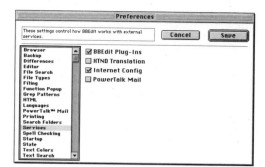

Figure 9.3 BBEdit's Services Preferences, where you'll tell BBEdit to work with Internet Config.

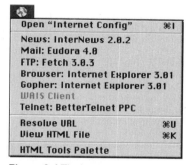

Figure 9.4 The Internet menu in BBEdit.

Configuring BBEdit to use Internet Config

Before you can use Internet Config in conjunction with BBEdit, you need to first be sure that BBEdit has been made aware of Internet Config. It can't hurt to double-check. You can follow these steps to find out for certain.

To configure BBEdit to work with Internet Config:

1. Launch BBEdit and open the Preferences.

2. Choose the Services portion of the Preferences and select the Internet Config option (see **Figure 9.3**).

3. Click the Save button.

If you've configured everything properly, you should see the Internet menu, as shown in **Figure 9.4**. If not, repeat the steps above and see the Internet Config home page for more information:

http://www.quinn.echidna.id.au/Quinn/Config/

How Internet Config works

Internet Config works by storing your preferences for Internet and miscellaneous applications and sharing that information with applications that request it. Most applications are not Internet Config–aware, but those that use the Internet do take advantage of Internet Config's services. For example, when you install a new software application it often asks you for your name and organization. If such an application is Internet Config–aware, it will enter this information for you by reading it from Internet Config's preferences.

Internet Config provides an interface to store these preferences, and the Internet Config Extension is actually the intermediary, accepting requests for the preferences and sending them to the applications that request the information.

The Internet Config application (see **Figure 9.5**) contains categories of information and interactivity with different kinds of applications that you'll need to configure to get BBEdit to work properly with your Internet applications.

✔ Tip

■ Some applications, such as Eudora Pro, can write to Internet Config as well as read from it.

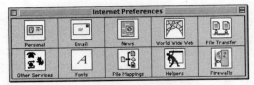

Figure 9.5 The main window of the Internet Config

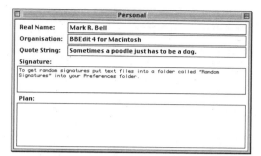

Figure 9.6 The Personal Preferences window of the Internet Config application.

Personal Preferences

The Personal Preferences section (see **Figure 9.6**) is where you'll enter information about yourself, for the benefit of those applications that request it.

To configure the Personal Preferences:

1. Launch Internet Config.

2. Click once on the Personal button.

3. Edit the fields as necessary.

4. Close the Personal window.

5. Choose File | Save (or Command+S) to save your changes.

When configuring this section, you may choose to edit any of the following fields:

1. Real Name

2. Organisation

3. Quote String

4. Signature

5. Plan

✔ Tip

■ The creators of Internet Config are from Australia, and they often use alternative spellings for words like organization, but that won't affect your Personal Preferences in any way.

PERSONAL PREFERENCES

Email Preferences

The Email Preferences section (see **Figure 9.7**) is where you'll enter information about your primary e-mail account. You may have more than one account, but Internet Config only keeps track of one account at this time.

To configure the Email Preferences:

1. Launch Internet Config.

2. Click once on the Email button.

3. Edit the fields as necessary.

4. Close the Email window.

5. Choose File | Save (or Command+S) to save your changes.

When configuring this section, you may choose to edit any of the following fields:

1. Email Address

2. Email Account

3. Email Password

4. SMTP Host

5. Email Headers

6. On New Mail

✔ Tip

■ Web browsers like Microsoft Internet Explorer will read the Mail Preferences to configure its their email preferences.

■ Eudora Pro will write to Internet Config with information on these preferences.

Figure 9.7 The Email Preferences window of the Internet Config application.

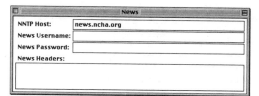

Figure 9.8 The News Preferences window of the Internet Config application.

News Preferences

The News Preferences section (see **Figure 9.8**) is where you'll enter information about your Usenet News service. Many people don't have access to Usenet, but most large organizations, universities, and Internet Service Providers (ISPs) do have access. Usenet uses the Network News Transfer Protocol (NNTP) to transfer messages between news servers, and you will have a client such as Netscape Navigator or InterNews to read the news.

To configure the News Preferences:

1. Launch Internet Config.

2. Click once on the News button.

3. Edit the fields as necessary.

4. Close the News window.

5. Choose File | Save (or Command+S) to save your changes.

When configuring this section, you may choose to edit any of the following fields:

1. NNTP Host

2. News Username

3. News Password

4. news Headers

✔ Tip

■ In case you don't know, Usenet was started at Duke University as a means of sharing information with its neighbors down the road at the University of North Carolina at Chapel Hill. It subsequently became very popular in the academic community.

NEWS PREFERENCES

World Wide Web Preferences

The World Wide Web Preferences section (see **Figure 9.9**) is where you'll enter information about your Web browsing preferences. Most Web browsers have several dozen configuration options at least, and this section of Internet Config is for just a few basic preferences.

Figure 9.9 The World Wide Web Preferences window of the Internet Config application.

To configure the World Wide Web Preferences:

1. Launch Internet Config.

2. Click once on the World Wide Web button.

3. Edit the fields as necessary.

4. Close the World Wide Web window.

5. Choose File | Save (or Command+S) to save your changes.

When configuring this section, you may choose to edit either of the following fields:

1. Home Page

2. Background Colour

✔ Tip

■ Some Web browsers that claim to be Internet Config–aware will not honor these preferences and will substitute their own preferences.

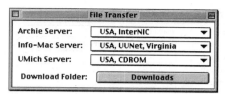

Figure 9.10 The File Transfer Preferences window of the Internet Config application.

File Transfer Preferences

The File Transfer Preferences section (see **Figure 9.10**) is where to look for commonly used download sites. You may not use all, or any, of these service and prefer instead to open up a Web browser and surf to your favorite download provider such as download.com.

To configure the File Transfer Preferences:

1. Launch Internet Config.

2. Click once on the File Transfer button.

3. Edit the fields as necessary.

4. Close the File Transfer window.

5. Choose File | Save (or Command+S) to save your changes.

When configuring this section, you may choose to edit any of the following fields:

1. Archie Server

2. Info-Mac Server

3. Umich Server

4. Download Folder

FILE TRANSFER PREFERENCES

Other Services Preferences

The Other Services Preferences section (see **Figure 9.11**) is where to look for several miscellaneous Internet services. Some of these service will be familiar to you, like with FTP and Gopher, but many of the other may not be important to you at all. If you don't know what these services are, don't worry about it. Just leave them blank.

To configure the Other Service Preferences:

1. Launch Internet Config.

2. Click once on the Other Services button.

3. Edit the fields as necessary.

4. Close the Other Services window.

5. Choose File | Save (or Command+S) to save your changes.

When configuring this section, you may choose to edit any of the following fields:

1. Ph Host

2. Finger Host

3. Whois Host

4. Telnet Host

5. FTP Host

6. Gopher Host

7. WAIS Gateway

8. LDAP Server

9. LDAP Searchbase

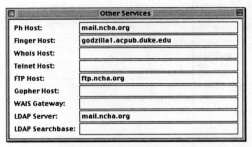

Figure 9.11 The Other Services Preferences window of the Internet Config application.

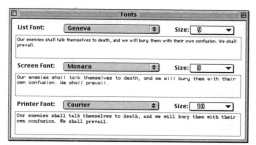

Figure 9.12 The Fonts Preferences window of the Internet Config application.

Font Preferences

The Font Preferences section (see **Figure 9.12**) is where you go to configure your screen and printer font options, including the font typeface and the size of the font.

To configure the Fonts Preferences:

1. Launch Internet Config.

2. Click once on the Fonts button.

3. Edit the fields as necessary.

4. Close the Fonts window.

5. Choose File | Save (or Command+S) to save your changes.

When configuring this section, you may choose to edit any of the following fields:

1. List Font

2. Screen Font

3. Printer Font

File Mapping Preferences

The File Mappings Preferences section (see **Figure 9.13**) is where you go to designate which application will open files with a specific file extension. This is really holdover from the MS-DOS world because on the Mac OS, you just double-click on an icon and let the OS launch the right application.

There are many options in this section, so don't worry about all the file types you don't recognize.

To configure the File Mappings Preferences:

1. Launch Internet Config.

2. Click once on the **File Mappings** button.

3. Edit the fields as necessary.

4. Close the **File Mappings** window.

5. Choose **File | Save** (or **Command+S**) to save your changes.

When configuring this section, select an entry and tell Internet Config what application you want to open it. You may also add new entries and delete the ones you no longer need.

✔ Tip

■ Be sure to identify BBEdit as the application for files ending in .htm as well as .html.

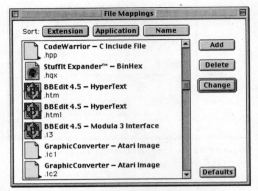

Figure 9.13 The File Mappings Preferences window of the Internet Config application.

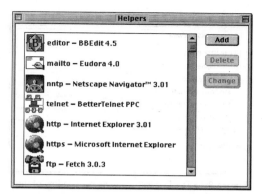

Figure 9.14 The Helpers Preferences window of the Internet Config application.

Helpers Preferences

The Helpers Preferences section (see **Figure 9.14**) is where you go to configure what helper application to use when requested by a Web browser. You will be most concerned with assigning a Web browser to view HTML documents, but more importantly you'll want to be sure to assign BBEdit as the text and HTML editor of choice (as in **Figure 9.14**).

To configure the Helpers Preferences:

1. Launch Internet Config.
2. Click once on the Helpers button.
3. Edit the fields as necessary.
4. Close the Helpers window.
5. Choose File | Save (or Command+S) to save your changes.

✔ Tip

■ Be sure to identify BBEdit as your editor!

Firewall Preferences

Finally, the Firewall Preferences section (see **Figure 9.15**) is where you go to configure your computer to use firewall services, usually for Web and FTP activity. Firewalls are used to provide security on Internet sites that contain important, valuable, or confidential data. The firewall helps to keep internal users in, and external users out.

To configure the Firewall Preferences:

1. Launch Internet Config.

2. Click once on the Firewalls button.

3. Edit the fields as necessary.

4. Close the Firewalls window.

5. Choose File | Save (or Command+S) to save your changes.

When configuring this section, you may choose to edit any of the following fields:

1. Use SOCK Firewall

2. Use HTTP Proxy

3. Use Gopher Proxy

4. Use FTP Proxy

5. FTP Proxy Username

6. FTP Proxy Password

7. FTP Proxy Account

8. FTP Using Passive Mode (PASV)

9. No Proxy For

✔ Tip

■ Firewalls tend to be very complicated, so if you know your Web site or ISP uses a firewall, check with your system administrator or ISP if you have concerns with any of these options.

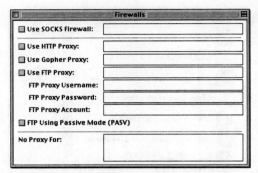

Figure 9.15 The Firewalls Preferences window of the Internet Config application.

FIREWALL PREFERENCES

10

SCRIPTING

BBEdit is a scriptable application, which means you can write small programs called *scripts* using AppleScript and Frontier to tell BBEdit to perform multiple tasks or execute useful shortcuts. You can make these scripts available to BBEdit through the Scripts menu, or you can launch them from the Finder or from other applications.

The power of controlling applications through scripting lies in the ability to effect a change on a large number of documents at once. This is vital for maintaining a large Web site, and most scripts of this type are implemented through AppleScript.

With Frontier, you can create shortcuts within BBEdit by defining aliases for commonly used data. An alias only has to typed once, but can be implemented as often as needed. Frontier offers other time-saving benefits, such as automatic enabling of URLs. Most of the scripts in this chapter can be implemented in either AppleScript or Frontier.

Scripting is a very different kind of task than authoring HTML documents because AppleScript and Frontier are object-oriented programming languages and are therefore very different from HTML. So, to make things a bit clearer, I'll use examples scripts to demonstrate the principles behind scripting as well as how scripting might be used to automate the most common tasks associated with authoring HTML documents.

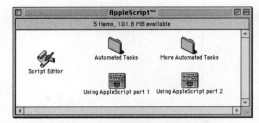

Figure 10.1 A standard AppleScript installation.

AppleScript

An AppleScript is just a list of instructions called *statements* that tell applications what to do. When the script is executed, the statements are sent to the AppleScript Extension, which in turn sends them to the correct application.

There are two ways of creating scripts. The first is to write the statements in a text editor such as BBEdit. The second is to record them by using the Script Editor program, which is included with the Mac OS (see **Figure 10.1**). Any script created with the Script Editor program is recognizable by the script icon. If the script was created with a text editor, open it with the Script Editor and then save it; it will then have the script icon and be recognized by the system as a script.

✔ Tips

■ The AppleScript Extension must be present in the Extensions folder in order for AppleScript to run.

■ AppleScript is a standard part of all versions of the Mac OS, but if you don't have it, visit the Apple Software Home Page at the following URL:

http://support.info.apple.com/ftp/swhome.html

Once you have created a script, you can run it with the Script Editor by clicking the Run button.

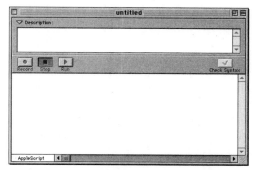

Figure 10.2 The Script Editor can be used to create new AppleScripts, as well as to convert text documents into AppleScripts.

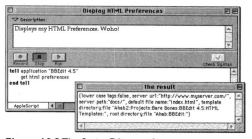

Figure 10.3 The Script Editor with an open script.

Creating a New Script

You use the Script Editor program to create new scripts, or alternatively, you can create the script with a text editor and then use Script Editor to change that text into a script.

To create a new script with Script Editor:

1. Choose File | New (or Command+N) for a new Script to be created within Script Editor, or

2. Choose File | Open Script (or Command+O) to open an existing script or a text document that contains AppleScript commands.

Selecting New will open an editor window like the one shown in **Figure 10.2**. Opening an existing script text document will result in the same window, but with the script written in the bottom section of the window. **Figure 10.3** shows a sample script that displays my HTML Preferences in the window entitled "the result."

Documenting the Script

It is important to document your scripts, because without documentation you'll have to go through all of the commands in the script to find out how it works. Documentation is especially useful when working with scripts that are not your own creation, or sharing scripts with others.

To document a script with the Script Editor:

1. Select File | New (or Command+N) to open a new editor window.

2. Type a description of the script in the top portion of the window (**Figure 10.4**).

✔ Tips

- It's nice to credit the author of a script in the Description field, or otherwise give credit where credit is due.

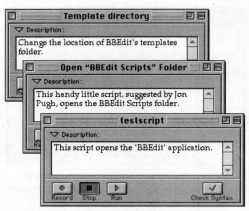

Figure 10.4 The description will help you keep track of what a script does.

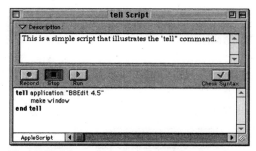

Figure 10.5 A very basic AppleScript illustrating the tell command.

Using the Tell Command

The tell command issues a command to an application. (The commands available for BBEdit will be covered later in the chapter.) The tell command specifies which application is to respond, and gives the application enough information to carry out the given task. The tell command is accompanied by an end tell command, which indicates when the AppleScript is no longer directing commands to the specified program. A sample of the tell command is illustrated in **Figure 10.5**.

To use the tell command in an AppleScript:

1. Open the Script Editor application.

2. If the script window is not already open, go to the File menu and choose New Script.

3. Type the following in the script window:

tell application "BBEdit 4.5"
    make window
end tell

Then save the script and click on the button marked Run to execute it.

Using AppleScript Dictionaries

Not all AppleScript commands can be used on all applications. To learn which AppleScript commands can be used on a particular application, look at that application's *dictionary*. This is a list of all commands, with short descriptions of how to use them.

To view an application's dictionary:

1. Choose File | Open Dictionary from the Script Editor menu bar.

2. From the dialog box that appears, choose the application whose dictionary you want to view, as shown in **Figure 10.6**.

3. Choose the command that you want to view from the list on the left side of the new window. The description of the command appears on the right side of the window, as shown in **Figure 10.7**.

4. You can display descriptions of a whole set of commands at once, as in **Figure 10.8**.

Notice that some of the commands are italicized. These commands are what is known as *object classes*, which are nothing more than groups of commands (see the "BBEdit object classes" section later in this chapter for an example).

To save the explanations of the commands and object classes to a text file, select a command or multiple commands by highlighting them and then choose File | Save As, the result of which is shown in **Figure 10.9**. This is useful if you need to reference the commands using BBEdit, or if you want to import them into a word processor.

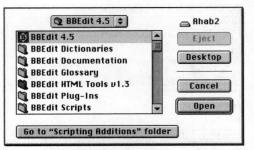

Figure 10.6 Pick an application.

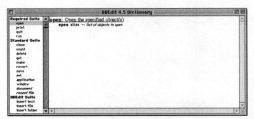

Figure 10.7 Click on a command to view its description.

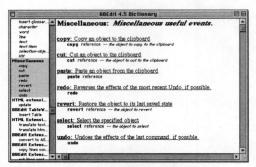

Figure 10.8 Click on the heading of a group of commands to view them all at once.

Figure 10.9 You can save the explanation of the commands to a text file for future reference.

Figure 10.10 The Required AppleScript suite.

Figure 10.11 The Standard AppleScript suite.

The Required Suite

The Required Suite (see **Figure 10.10**) is a list of commands that should be available in every application that is scriptable using AppleScript. It is derived from Apple's *Human Interface Guidelines*, which states that these commands should be in every Apple application. Each italicized word below represents a variable that should be replaced by an appropriate name.

open *filename* tells the application to open *filename*, which can be one or more specified documents.

print *filename* tells the application to print *filename*, which can be one or more specified documents.

quit tells the application to quit.

run tells the application to begin executing, as when its icon is double-clicked.

The Standard Suite

The Standard Suite (see **Figure 10.11**) is a list of commands common to most applications that are scriptable with AppleScript. The Standard Suite is too large to be listed here, but here are some common commands:

close *windowname* this closes the window named by *windowname*.

delete *itemname* this deletes the item named by *itemname*.

save *windowname* to *filename* this saves the contents of the window named by *windowname* to the file named by *filename*.

The BBEdit Suite

As with all scriptable applications, BBEdit has its own scripting commands. The BBEdit Suite (see **Figure 10.12**) defines its many scripting commands to make them easier to use. With these commands, you can perform simple tasks, such as inserting text into documents, as well as more complex tasks, such as performing searches. The many subsets of the BBEdit suite perform tasks ranging from automatic formatting of text into HTML to cutting and pasting text between groups of documents. Finally, there are commands derived from extensions that can be added to BBEdit. These commands will differ depending on which extensions are currently installed. The commands are as follows:

- **insert text** inserts literal text.
- **insert file** inserts the contents of the designated file.
- **insert folder** inserts the file names of the contents of the designated folder.
- **insert project** inserts the file list of a Think Project Manager, Think Pascal, or CodeWarrior project.
- **find** searches for text in the front window, or optionally in multiple files.
- **replace** replaces either the selection or all occurrences.
- **find differences** finds and displays differences between two files, folders, or projects.
- **go to line** places the insertion point at the start of the selected line.
- **go to function** selects the text indicated by the designated function name (source files only).
- **go to marker** selects the text indicated by the designated marker.
- **select current paragraph** selects the paragraph surrounding the current insertion point (or selection range).

Figure 10.12 The BBEdit Suite of scripting commands.

- **twiddle** exchanges the first and last characters of the selection range, or the two characters directly adjacent to the insertion point.
- **change case** changes the case of text in an editing window.
- **shift** shifts the selected text left or right, optionally by one space.
- **hard wrap** hard wraps the text (or the text of the current selection) to conform to the parameters.
- **insert line breaks** inserts a hard line break character at the end of each soft-wrapped line.
- **remove line breaks** removes hard line-break characters from a document, making it suitable for soft-wrapping.
- **unwrap** removes extra carriage returns and white space from the document.
- **zap gremlins** removes or replaces unwanted characters from the text in the current window.
- **entab** replaces runs of spaces with tabs.
- **detab** replaces tabs with runs of spaces.
- **insert glossary entry** inserts the specified glossary entry into the front editing window.

BBEdit Object Classes

The following objects classes are also part of the BBEdit suite, with each object class having multiple elements and properties.

Class character

a character

Plural form:

characters

Elements:

character by numeric index

'cins' before/after another element

text as a range of elements

text item by numeric index

word by numeric index

Properties:

length integer

offset integer

startLine integer

endLine integer

startColumn integer

endColumn integer

Class word

a word

Plural form:

words

Elements:

character by numeric index

'cins' before/after another element

text as a range of elements

text item by numeric index

word by numeric index

Properties:

length integer

offset integer

startLine integer

endLine integer

startColumn integer

endColumn integer

Class line

a line

Plural form:

lines

Elements:

character by numeric index

line by numeric index

text as a range of elements

word by numeric index

Properties:

length integer

offset integer

endLine integer

startColumn integer

endColumn integer

Class text

text

Elements:

character by numeric index

'cins' before/after another element

text as a range of elements

text item by numeric index

word by numeric index

line by numeric index

Properties:

length integer

offset integer

startLine integer

endLine integer

startColumn integer

endColumn integer

Class text item

a text item

Plural form:

text items

Elements:

character by numeric index

'cins' before/after another element

text as a range of elements

text item by numeric index

word by numeric index

Properties:

length integer

offset integer

startLine integer

endLine integer

startColumn integer

endColumn integer

Class selection-object

the selected text

Elements:

character by numeric index

line by numeric index

'cpar' by numeric index

text as a range of elements

word by numeric index

Properties:

contents type class

length integer

offset integer

startLine integer

endLine integer

startColumn integer

endColumn integer

Class Hit

describes a multi-file search hit

Properties:

file file specification

line integer

start integer

end integer

context string

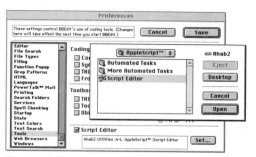

Figure 10.13 Selecting a script editor.

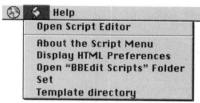

Figure 10.14 The script editor available from the Scripts menu.

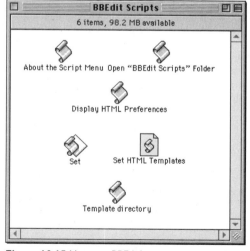

Figure 10.15 Home to BBEdit's scripts.

Making Your Scripts Available in BBEdit

Elsewhere in this book, you've read about accessing your scripts from within BBEdit. Here are more detailed instructions.

To identify a script editor and make scripts available in BBEdit:

1. Open your Preferences.

2. Go to the Tools section, check the Script Editor checkbox, and select a script editor such as AppleScript (see **Figure 10.13**).

3. Close and save the Preferences.

4. Go to the Scripts menu and verify that a script editor is available (see **Figure 10.4**).

5. Put your scripts in a folder called BBEdit Scripts within the same folder as BBEdit (see **Figure 10.15**).

Example: Prompt the User to Select a Folder

This is an example of how to query the user for a folder, and then to perform a certain action on each file in that folder. The action, sending the files to a PostScript printer, was arbitrarily chosen from the BBEdit Extension Suite, and could be replaced by any other action as defined in the BBEdit Script Dictionary. This example relates to the one that follows it.

To prompt a user to select a folder:

1. Open the Script Editor.

2. Type the following:

```
tell application "Finder"
    activate
    copy (choose folder) to sourceFolder
```

3. Save the script.

This tells AppleScript to give the user a dialog box from which to select a folder. For the rest of the program, the name of the folder is referred to as sourceFolder.

Note that I used a **tell** command without using the corresponding **end tell** that was mentioned earlier in this chapter. That's because this script continues into the next section, and the **end tell** statement is at the end of that script.

Example: Performing an Action on Each Element of a Folder

This is a continuation of the last script, with which you opened a folder. Now you're ready to do something to the files within that folder.

In this instance, you're encasing the action in a loop. This is a programming concept that refers to performing an action many times. The number of files in the folder chosen by the user tells the script how many times to repeat the action.

Sending every file in a folder to a PostScript printer:

1. Continue the script in the last example by typing in the following:

```
set fileQuantity to count files in sourceFolder
repeat with myLoop from 1 to fileQuantity
    set theFile to item myLoop of sourceFolder
    set theFileType to file type obsolete
    → of theFile
    if theFileType is "TEXT" then tell
    → application "BBEdit 4.5"
        activate
            open theFile
            send PostScript
        end tell
    end repeat
end tell
```

This script starts with a directive to AppleScript to count the number of files in the selected folder, and then to assign that number to a variable called fileQuantity. The fileQuantity variable is used in the next statement to go to each file in the selected folder.

The script checks the file type of the current file by using a variable called **fileType**. Like the **fileQuantity** variable, this name was chosen solely to help us remember what the variable does, not because it has any special properties. The variable name could just as well have been x or y. The important words in that statement were the set, file type, and obsolete. The syntax of these commands can be found in the Scripting Dictionaries.

Once the file type of the current file has been checked, the text files are opened in BBEdit. They are then printed with the command **send PostScript**. Any other command or set of Commands could have been inserted at this point; the **sendPostScript** command was chosen solely as a demonstration.

Example: Getting Input from Users

Printing isn't a very useful function when you're designing a Web site, but the previous example makes a useful illustration of scripting because it is a function that only takes one line to write. The function in the next example takes several lines, but could just as easily be inserted in the middle of the previous example.

This is a shortcut for the find and replace operation, and it also shows you how to get input from the user in the form of a dialog box. The user selects a word, runs the script, and is then prompted to type in a new word. The script will replace each occurrence of the selected word with the new one. If you insert the relevant statements into the example above, the user will be able to execute a replace-text command on many files at once. You can customize the dialog box, specifying the name of the dialog, the buttons, and default text.

To use the replace text script:

1. Open the Script Editor.

2. Enter the following text:

```
tell application "BBEdit 4.5"
    activate
    set userAnswer to display dialog ¬
        "Enter the new Word"
        buttons {"Cancel","OK"} ¬
        default button "OK" ¬
        default answer " "
    set newWord to text returned of userAnswer
    set oldWord to selected text
    replace Every Occurrence ¬
    searching for oldWord ¬
        case sensitive false ¬
        using newWord
    return
end tell
```

Frontier

UserLand Frontier (see **Figure 10.16**), a tool included on the BBEdit CD-ROM, is also an object-oriented programming language and uses scripting and object management to automate the process of creating and managing large Web sites. It is a complement to, but not a replacement for, AppleScript and works with many applications, especially BBEdit.

As an Object Database, Frontier stores objects such as text and HTML commands so you don't have to type them repeatedly as you create a Web site. This is useful, for example, if you decide to change a particular element of an HTML document that appears in many places on your Web site. With Frontier, you can just change the object in the Object Database, and with the click of the mouse, recreate the entire Web site, a process called *rendering*.

In addition to storing objects such as text and HTML commands, Frontier can also store other scripts. For example, you can create a script that performs a calculation, such as calculate a daily interest rate or the value of an investment, then have that value automatically inserted into a particular Web page. This is known as a *macro*. Macros can be written in Frontier, or they can be in AppleScript then called by a Frontier script. Indeed, many people use AppleScript in conjunction with Frontier to maintain Web sites.

✔ Tip

■ For the latest information and download links, see the following URL:

http://www.scripting.com/frontier

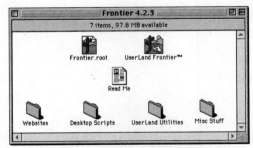

Figure 10.16 UserLand Frontier as installed by the BBEdit installation program.

FRONTIER

Installing Frontier

Frontier is not automatically installed as part of the BBEdit installation routine, even using the Custom Install option. So, you'll need to follow these steps in order to install Frontier and to allow for full cooperation between Frontier and BBEdit.

1. Copy the entire Frontier folder to your hard drive from the BBEdit CD-ROM, or download the latest version from the Frontier Web site and decompress it.

2. Open the folder entitled Misc Stuff:Copy to System Folder and move the IdleTime and OSA Menu Extensions to the Extensions folder inside your System Folder.

3. Restart your computer.

INSTALLING FRONTIER

Accessing Frontier from BBEdit

Now that you have installed Frontier, you can easily access Frontier from within BBEdit. The Frontier installation adds two new items to the menu bar of BBEdit from which you can execute scripts or get values from the Frontier Object Database.

To configure BBEdit to work with Frontier:

1. Launch BBEdit.

2. Open the Preferences by choosing Edit | Preferences (or Command+;) and select the Tools section (see **Figure 10.17**).

3. Select the Frontier checkbox.

4. Click the Save button and quit BBEdit.

To open Frontier from within BBEdit:

1. Choose Open Frontier from the newly added Frontier menu (see **Figure 10.18**).

2. Once Frontier has been launched, you can then choose one of the Frontier commands from the Site menu, which only appears if Frontier is running at the same time as BBEdit (see **Figure 10.19**).

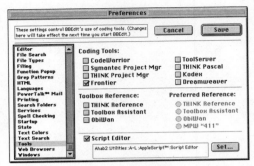

Figure 10.17 Configuring BBEdit to work with Frontier requires that you choose the Frontier option in the Tools Preferences.

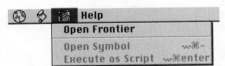

Figure 10.18 The Frontier menu.

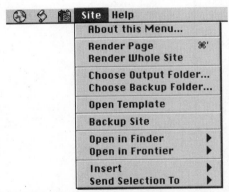

Figure 10.19 The Site menu, which appears when Frontier is running at the same time as BBEdit.

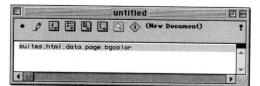

Figure 10.20 Frontier can act on a phrase within a BBEdit document like this.

Figure 10.21 Your first look into the Frontier Object Database.

Using the Object Database

Frontier's Object Database is where objects such as HTML formatting commands and text are stored for use in Web pages. These objects can be accessed directly through Frontier, or from within BBEdit. The following example illustrates Frontier stores the color white (FFFFFF) as a background color in the Object Database, which will help you understand the structure and uses of the Object Database.

To access the Object Database:

1. Open a new BBEdit document.

2. Type suites.html.data.page.bgcolor.

3. Select the words you just typed, as in **Figure 10.20**.

4. Choose Open Symbol from BBEdit's Frontier menu.

This opens the Frontier database to the location where this value is stored. You can see what this looks like in **Figure 10.21**, where the term bgcolor is stored as a string of characters and equals FFFFFF. In the next example, you'll see how to use Frontier to automatically insert this value into a BBEdit document.

Getting a Value from the Object Database

In the previous example, you opened the database to see a value stored within. The following example shows you how to use the power of scripting to bring that value directly into a BBEdit document.

To get a value from the Object Database:

1. Open a new BBEdit document.

2. Type suites.html.data.page.bgcolor.

3. Select the words you just typed.

4. Choose Execute Script from BBEdit's Frontier menu.

This will enter the value stored in the suites.html.data.page.bgcolor location of the Object Database into your BBEdit document. You should see something similar to **Figure 10.22**.

To perform a calculation:

Besides opening pre-stored values, this technique can also be used to perform a calculation.

1. Open a new BBEdit document.

2. Type x=20+2.

3. Select the numbers you just typed.

4. Choose Execute Script from BBEdit's Frontier menu.

The result of this calculation is shown in **Figure 10.23**.

Figure 10.22 Retrieving an entry from the Object Database.

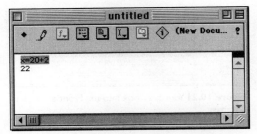

Figure 10.23 Executing a calculation in BBEdit using Frontier.

Figure 10.24 A list of links that I might want to put on many pages, but that might change at any time.

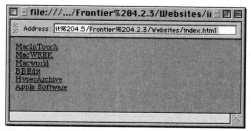

Figure 10.25 The result of using a template and rendering the page using Frontier.

Using Templates

The power of Frontier is not fully realized until you begin to use templates. A template can be defined by determining a common theme for all of your Web pages. Every Web site has at least one template called #template.html.

The template files contain HTML code, which is inserted into pages wherever the template is used. The template is "summoned" by putting its name (without the # symbol) in a pair of curly braces {}. Frontier will take the entire body of the template and insert it in place of the word in the curly braces, much the way BBEdit uses placeholders and file includes.

To create and use a sample template:

1. Create a new document called #template.html.

2. Enter some HTML data, such as the list of hyperlinks in **Figure 10.24**.

3. Save and close the document.

4. Create another document called index.html, and store it in the same folder as the #template.html file.

5. Type {links} in the document, which is Frontier's instruction to insert the contents of #template.html.

6. Save the document.

7. Choose Site | Render Page.

Frontier will automatically create a new document called index.html inside a folder called Websites in the Frontier folder, then issue the Preview command to BBEdit, causing it to open the newly created document in a Web browser (see **Figure 10.25**).

USING TEMPLATES

Using the Glossary

The glossary is a Frontier table that contains definitions of terms, much like a placeholder in BBEdit. Glossary entries are contained in double-quotes, and are exchanged for their definitions whenever a page is rendered using Frontier. In other words, the rendering process exchanges the glossary entries for their definitions, making the glossary yet another way to make shortcuts using Frontier.

Suppose you refer to a certain word or sentence many times in your Web pages. You might not want to type this phrase every time you come to it. Or if the phrase is a slogan, catch phrase, or piece other corporate nomenclature, it might change, in which case it would be important to update every occurrence. A good example of this is with hyperlinks. They take too long to type in, and if the location of a site changes, you don't want to have to search all of your Web sites to make the change. The glossary can simplify all of these situations because it take the repetitiveness out of having to type this data over and over.

To use the glossary:

1. Choose Site | Open In Frontier | Glossary.

2. When the Frontier Glossary opens, choose Table | New Scalar | String.

3. Choose a small name for your entry, with just a few letters.

4. Enter a long sentence for the value, such as the one in **Figure 10.26**.

5. Change a previous HTML file to contain the name of the your entry in quotation marks, as in **Figure 10.27**.

6. Choose Scripts | BBEdit | Preview Page from your Web browser. Your default Web browser will open with the value of the glossary item, as in Figure 10.28.

Figure 10.26 Putting a value into the glossary.

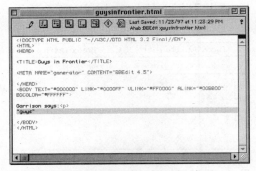

Figure 10.27 Getting the value from the glossary into a page.

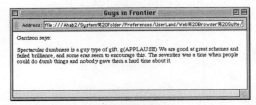

Figure 10.28 Previewing the result.

Frontier inserts your custom glossary entry to any document that references it, and because Frontier uses an object-oriented database to store its glossary entries, you can create highly complex Web sites using both the Object Database and the glossary. These examples only scratch the surface, but it you have the time to learn how to use Frontier, you can exercise new power over your Web sites using BBEdit and Frontier.

USING THE GLOSSARY

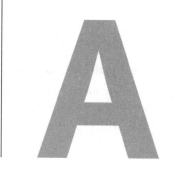

APPENDIX A: MENU ITEMS

Below are the BBEdit menu items as they appear when you choose them using the mouse alone, and when you hold down the Shift or Option keys. Some, but not all, of these menu options have keyboard equivalents, which can be seen in the figures.

Figure A.1 The BBEdit menu bar.

BBEdit Menu Bar

The BBEdit 4.5 menu bar contains the following items (see **Figure A.1**):

Apple—contains information about the creators of BBEdit and how to contact them.

File—performs file-manipulation tasks such as opening, saving, and printing.

Edit—performs editing functions such as cut, copy, paste, and undo, and contains the preferences for BBEdit.

Text—provides formatting changes to the text (changing case, tabs, and fonts).

Markers—allows the user to set and remove bookmarks in the document.

Search—contains extensive tools for finding and replacing items.

Tools—provides utilities that simplify or reduce work in the document.

Windows—provides access to multiple documents with BBEdit.

Internet (globe)—provides access to applications configured by the Internet Config program, as well as a few miscellaneous Web-related utilities and the HTML Tools palette.

Script—provides access to ready-made AppleScripts as well as the AppleScript editor.

Help—contains information on how to perform various functions and tasks in BBEdit.

Application menu—allows quick access to other programs running in conjunction with BBEdit.

The Apple Menu

The Apple menu (see **Figure A.2**) contains three items that provide information about BBEdit and how to contact the developer, Bare Bones Software.

About BBEdit—provides information about the developers of BBEdit, how to contact them, and memory usage.

Send us mail—launches a blank e-mail message addressed to Bare Bones Software.

Visit our Web Site—launches a Web browser by accessing the Bare Bones Software Web site.

The File Menu (DEFAULT VIEW)

The File menu (**Figure A.3**) contains options for organizing and manipulating files. As with other BBEdit menus, this menu has different options when the Shift or Option keys are held down while opening it.

File New—contains several file options for creating a new document.

New Text Document—opens a new untitled document window.

New (with selection)—inserts selected text from a previous document into a new document window.

New (with clipboard)—inserts contents of clipboard into a new document window.

New HTML document—creates a new document with basic HTML tags.

New PowerTalk letter—opens a new PowerTalk letter.

New File Group—creates a new group for files.

New Disk Browser—opens a new disk browser to view the contents of a volume.

Open—opens existing files.

Open from FTP Server—opens files located on remote servers.

Figure A.2 The Apple menu.

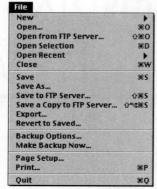

Figure A.3 The default File menu.

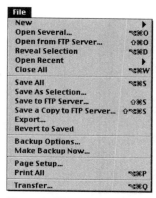

Figure A.4 The File menu with Option key pressed.

Open Selection—locates and opens a file that matches the selected text in an open window.

Open Recent—provides quick access to recently opened documents.

Close—closes active document window.

Save—writes active document to user-selected volume and location.

Save As—allows user to change the name of an existing document or save the document to a new location.

Save to FTP Server—saves active document to a remote server.

Save a Copy to FTP Server—saves a copy of the active document to a remote server.

Export—allows the user to save a document in another word processing format.

Revert to Saved—restores an active document to a previously saved version (warns first).

Backup Options—creates a backup copy of a document before saving changes.

Make Backup Now—makes a backup of the active document including changes.

Page Setup—sets printing options including orientation and paper size.

Print—prints active document.

Quit—exits BBEdit.

The File Menu (WITH OPTION KEY PRESSED)

The options shown in **Figure A.4** are accessed by holding down the Option key while using the mouse to open the File menu.

Open Several—opens more than one file.

Reveal Selection—reveals location of file in Finder when text selected in a document window is a file name.

Close All—closes all document windows.

Save All—saves changes made to all open documents.

Save as Selection—uses selected text in document window as the file name.

Revert to Saved—restores an active document to a previously saved version (no warning).

Print All—prints all open documents.

Transfer—quits BBEdit to launch another program.

The File Menu (WITH SHIFT KEY PRESSED)

The File menu options shown in **Figure A.5** are accessed by holding down the Shift key while using the mouse to open the File menu.

Close & Delete—closes an active PowerTalk letter and moves it to the trash.

Print One Copy—skips the printing dialog box and prints one copy of the active document.

The Edit Menu (DEFAULT VIEW)

The Edit menu is used for editing functions. It also contains important BBEdit preferences and options. Refer to **Figure A.6**.

Undo—negates previous action (typing, replacing, etc.).

Redo—restores an undone action.

Cut—removes selection and places it on the clipboard.

Copy—copies selection and places it on the clipboard.

Paste—inserts clipboard item at selection point.

Clear—removes selection.

Select All—selects entire document.

Select Line—selects line containing cursor.

Insert—brings up the primary menu for several insertion options.

    Insert File—pastes the contents of a selected file into the active document.

    Insert Folder Listing—inserts a directory and file listing of a selected folder.

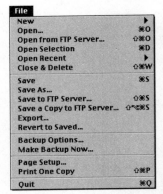

Figure A.5 The File menu with Shift key pressed.

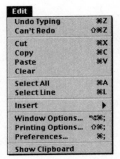

Figure A.6 The Edit menu.

MENU ITEMS

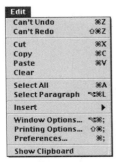

Figure A.7 The Edit menu with Option key pressed.

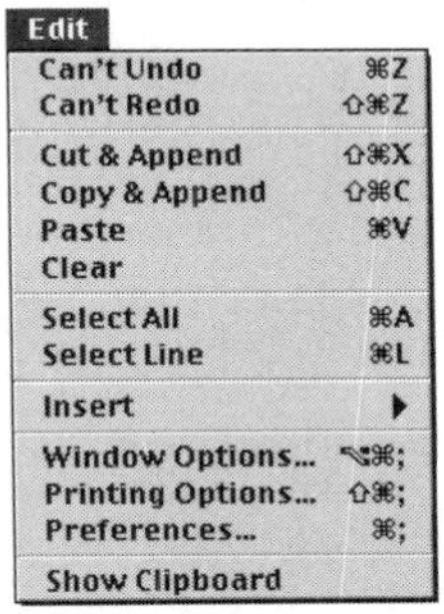

Figure A.8 The Edit menu with Shift key pressed.

Insert Project Listing—inserts a text listing of a selected project.

Insert Toolbox Call Template—creates new tools by using selected text to name the tool (brings up call template).

Insert Page Break—inserts a page break at the cursor.

Insert Selected Glossary Entry—inserts entry from glossary into document window.

Window Options—provides several options for the active document such as auto-indention, soft-wrapping text, color-coded programming, displaying hidden characters, and status bars.

Printing Options—sets options for printing the active document such as font, date stamps, and printing line numbers.

Preferences—sets preferences for BBEdit (see Appendix B).

Show Clipboard—displays contents of clipboard.

The Edit Menu (WITH OPTION KEY PRESSED)

The Edit menu item shown in **Figure A.7** is displayed when the Option key is pressed while using the mouse to open the Edit menu.

Select Paragraph—selects paragraph containing cursor (previously Select Line).

The Edit Menu (WITH SHIFT KEY PRESSED)

The Edit Menu items shown in **Figure A.8** are displayed when the Shift key is pressed while using the mouse to open the Edit menu.

Cut & Append—removes the selected text and adds it to the clipboard contents.

Copy & Append—copies the selected text and adds it to the clipboard contents.

MENU ITEMS

The Text Menu (DEFAULT VIEW)

The Text menu shown in **Figure A.9** provides options for formatting the document and text.

Font & Tabs—determines font, font style, and tab stops for document.

Balance—selects the text between parentheses or brackets.

Twiddle—reverses the characters at the cursor insertion point or at the ends of a selection.

Change Case—changes the case of selected text based on user choices.

Shift Left—moves selected text to the left one tab stop.

Shift Right—moves selected text to the right one tab stop.

Inserts Line Breaks—puts a line break at the end of every line.

Remove Line Breaks—removes line breaks in a selection or in entire document.

Hard Wrap—inserts line breaks at the ends of lines based on user-selected options.

Zap "Gremlins"—removes selected non-printing characters according to user options.

Entab—replaces groups of spaces with tabs.

Detab—replaces tabs with spaces.

Check Spelling—runs a spell check on the active document.

The Text Menu (WITH OPTION KEY PRESSED)

The Text menu options shown in **Figure A.10** are displayed when the Option key is pressed while using the mouse to open the Text menu.

Printing Font—sets font for the document.

Twiddle Words—reverses words at the cursor insertion point or at the ends of the selection.

Change Case—changes case based on the last option selected in the dialog box.

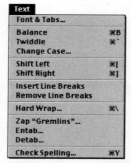

Figure A.9 The Text menu (default view).

Figure A.10 The Text menu with Option key pressed.

Figure A.11 The Text menu with Shift key pressed.

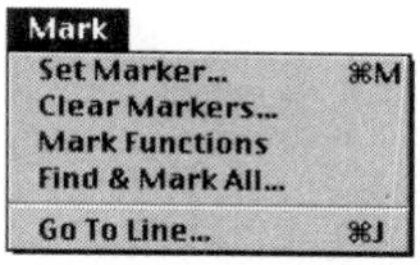

Figure A.12 The Mark menu (default view).

Hard Wrap—inserts line breaks at the ends of lines based on the last option selected in the dialog box.

Zap "Gremlins"—removes selected non-printing characters based on last option selected in the dialog box.

Entab—replaces groups of spaces with tabs based on last option selected in the dialog box.

Detab—replaces tabs with spaces based on last option selected in the dialog box.

The Text Menu (WITH SHIFT KEY PRESSED)

The Text menu options shown in **Figure A.11** are displayed when the Shift key is pressed while using the mouse to open the Text menu.

Shift Left One Space—moves selected text to the left one space.

Shift Right One Space—moves selected text to the right one space.

The Mark Menu (DEFAULT VIEW)

The Mark menu provides a way to navigate large files quickly by setting markers throughout the document (see **Figure A.12**).

Set Marker—offers the option of attaching a name to a section in a document.

Clear Markers—allows certain markers to be removed.

Mark Functions—sets markers at functions in the document.

Find & Mark All—based on a grep pattern, marks several selections in a document.

Go To Line—goes to a specific line.

MENU ITEMS

The Mark Menu (WITH OPTION KEY PRESSED)

The Mark menu options shown in **Figure A.13** are displayed when the Option key is pressed while using the mouse to open the Mark menu.

Set Marker—sets marker based on selected text name.

Clear All Markers—removes all markers in a document.

Go To Line—go to beginning of the line specified by the selected text.

The Mark Menu (WITH SHIFT KEY PRESSED)

The Mark menu option shown in **Figure A.14** is displayed when the Shift key is pressed while using the mouse to open the Mark menu.

Go To Center Line—moves cursor to the beginning of the line in the middle of the window.

The Search Menu (DEFAULT VIEW)

The Search menu provides options for locating and/or replacing items in a document (see **Figure A.15**).

Find—multipurpose dialog box that allows text to be located and replaced even over multiple files.

Find Again—performs an additional search based on the previous text string.

Find Selection—searches an active document based on selected text.

Enter Search String—performs a search based on selected text.

Replace—removes selected text and inserts replacement text string.

Replace All—removes all occurrences of search string and inserts replacement text string.

Figure A.13 The Mark menu with Option key pressed.

Figure A.14 The Mark menu with Shift key pressed.

Figure A.15 The Search menu (default view).

Figure A.16 The Search menu with Option key pressed

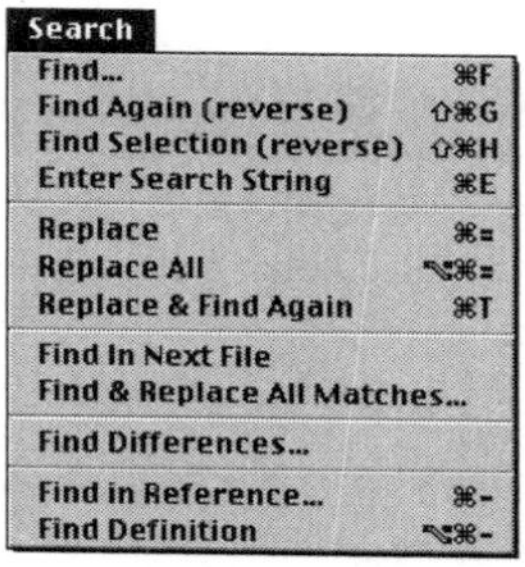

Figure A.17 The Search menu with Shift key pressed

Replace & Find Again—replaces search string in steps.

Find in Next File—performs search in next file selected in the Find dialog box.

Find & Replace All Matches replaces occurrences of search string with replacement text string over multiple files.

Find Differences—displays differences between two text files.

Find in Reference—allows search in Toolbox reference.

Find Definition—allows search of a database to define a symbol or function.

The Search Menu (WITH OPTION KEY PRESSED)

The Search menu options shown in **Figure A.16** are displayed when the Option key is pressed while using the mouse to open the Search menu.

Enter Replace String—uses selected text as replacement text string.

Open All Matches—opens all files that contain the search string.

The Search Menu (WITH SHIFT KEY PRESSED)

The Search menu options shown in **Figure A.17** are displayed when the Shift key is pressed while using the mouse to open the Search menu.

Find Again—performs additional search "backwards" in the document based on previous text string.

Find Selection—performs search "backwards" in active document based on selected text.

The Tools Menu

The Tools menu contains numerous functions that make creating specialized files such as HTML documents easier.

Tools List—plug-ins for HTML Tools in the upper half of the menu (**Figure A.18**) and miscellaneous functions in the lower half (**Figure A.19**).

The Windows Menu

Use the Windows Menu (**Figure A.20**) to access various open documents as well as the glossary.

Glossary—database the user can access and edit to insert entries in a document.

Compile Errors—brings up a window that displays compiler errors.

Quick Search—allows a character-based simple search of the active document.

Window List—opens a window indicating all open windows.

ASCII Table—brings up a window showing the ASCII character table.

Arrange—neatly arranges open document windows.

Get Info—provides information about the active document.

Reveal in Finder—reveals active document in Finder.

Send To Back—sends current window to back.

Exchange With Next—brings window second in line to the front.

Synchro Scrolling—scrolling in foremost windows is synchronized.

Figure A.18 The HTML functions on the Tools menu

Figure A.19 The miscellaneous functions on the Tools menu

Figure A.20 The Windows menu

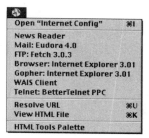

Figure A.21 The Internet menu

Figure A.22 The Script menu

The Internet Menu

The Internet menu (see **Figure A.21**) provides quick access to several Internet tools. These menu options will vary based on your configuration.

Open Internet Config—opens the program Internet Config.

News Reader, Mail, FTP, etc.—opens Internet functions that utilize various helper applications.

Resolve URL—verifies the accuracy of a URL reference within a text selection.

View HTML File—views the contents of an HTML file in a Web browser.

Open HTML Tools Palette—opens a window containing HTML tools.

The Script Menu

The Script menu provides access to AppleScripts and the AppleScript editor (see **Figure A.22**).

Open Script Editor—opens the Macintosh AppleScript Editor.

About the Script Menu—runs a sample AppleScript.

Open "BBEdit Scripts" Folder—an AppleScript that opens the folder containing BBEdit scripts.

The Help Menu

Use the Help Menu shown in **Figure A.23** to get access to online and instant help resources.

About BBEdit Guide—information about the contents of the BBEdit Apple guide.

Show/Hide Balloons—toggle menu that turns on/off balloon help.

BBEdit Guide—online help database based on the Apple Guide format.

What's New—Apple Guide listing new features in BBEdit 4.5.

The Application Menu

This menu is a standard Macintosh menu. The items relating to BBEdit 4.5 follow (see **Figure A.24**).

Hide BBEdit 4.5—places BBEdit 4.5 in the background and hides open windows.

Hide Others—hides other running applications and shows only BBEdit.

Show All—makes all running applications visible.

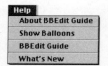

Figure A.23 The Help menu

Figure A.24 The Application menu

MENU ITEMS

APPENDIX B: PREFERENCES

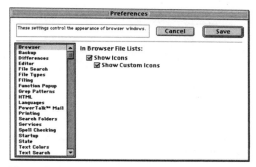

Figure B.1 The Browser Preferences window.

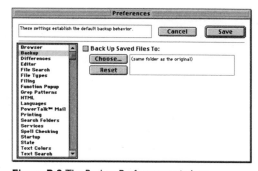

Figure B.2 The Backup Preferences window.

Preferences set the stage for the performance of BBEdit. One of best things about BBEdit is the wide variety of preference settings available to the user. And most importantly, the Preferences are all located in one dialog box under the Edit menu, so you don't have to worry about chasing down configuration options in multiple locations.

Browser (Figure B.1)

Show Icons—determines whether icons are displayed in the disk browser window.

Show Custom Icons—determines whether custom or generic icons are displayed.

Backup (Figure B.2)

Back Up Saved Files To:—sets the backup as default action.

Choose—allows the selection of a backup folder.

Reset—saves backup files to same folder as original document.

Differences (Figure B.3)

Compare Options—determines comparison criteria such as Case Sensitive and Ignore Leading Space when using the Difference menu option.

Place Windows On—determines where the results will be displayed including a second screen (if one is attached).

Relative Placement—determines location of comparison and results windows.

Editor (Figure B.4)

Default Font—sets default font, font size, and tab stops for BBEdit 4.5.

Auto-Indent—indents new lines automatically.

Balance While Typing—flashes opening parenthesis or bracket in a sentence when the closing parenthesis or bracket is typed.

Smart Quotes—turns apostrophes and quotation marks into printer's quotes.

Smart Editing—eliminates extra spaces when pasting selections.

Show Invisibles/Show Spaces—shows hidden characters (can be configured to show only spaces).

Auto-Expand Tabs—adds adequate spaces to reach next tab stop without typing the tab character.

Syntax Coloring—color codes programming language within the document.

Soft Wrap—wraps text within window based upon user choice of Philip bar, window width, or set character width.

Keypad Cursor Controls—enables cursor movement via the keypad.

Exchange Command and Option—exchanges the function of the Command and Option keys.

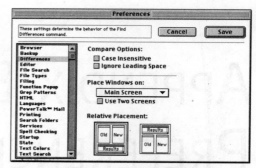

Figure B.3 The Differences Preferences window.

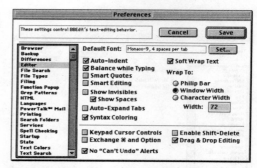

Figure B.4 The Editor Preferences window.

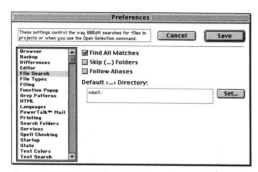

Figure B.5 The File Search Preferences window.

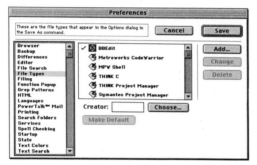

Figure B.6 The File Types Preferences window.

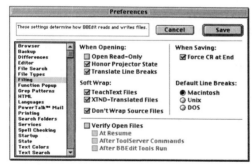

Figure B.7 The Filing Preferences window.

No "Can't Undo" Alerts—disables the warning that a chosen action cannot be undone.

Enable Shift-Delete—enables forward deleting by using the shift-delete key combination.

Drag-and-Drop Editing—allows selected text to be selected and moved by mouse.

File Search (Figure B.5)

Find All Matches—shows all files that match the search criteria.

Skip ( ) Folder—skips files enclosed by parentheses when doing a file search.

Follow Aliases—locate the alias originals when searching.

Default < > Directory—when text is enclosed by < >, will search the directory designated here.

File Types (Figure B.6)

This preference contains all file types that are recognized by BBEdit. New types can be added.

Filing (Figure B.7)

Open Read Only—when opening files, changes cannot be made to file.

Honor Projector State—when opening file, BBEdit upholds projector states that indicate a file cannot be edited.

Translate Line Breaks—when opening file, changes Unix and DOS line breaks to Macintosh line breaks.

TeachText Files—soft wrap files created in TeachText.

XTND-Translated Files—soft wraps files translated by XTND.

Don't Wrap Source Files—overrides soft wrap settings for source files.

PREFERENCES

When Saving, Force CR at End—ensures a line break is at the end of a file.

Default Line Breaks—sets style of line breaks, whether Macintosh, Unix, or DOS.

Verify Open Files—provides options for determining whether a file open in BBEdit has been modified by another application.

Function Popup (Figure B.8)

This preference determines how functions are displayed in the Tool menu and is beyond the scope of this book.

Grep Patterns (Figure B.9)

This preference contains saved grep searches and can be edited to include new patterns as well as remove old ones.

HTML (Figure B.10)

HTML Tags—sets default case for HTML tags (choices are upper or lower case).

Server—contains the default server for user HTML files.

Path—saves the default path for the HTML files on the remote server.

Default Name—indicates default name of new HTML documents.

Root—allows user to set root directory to enable relative paths.

Template—indicates template to be used for new HTML files.

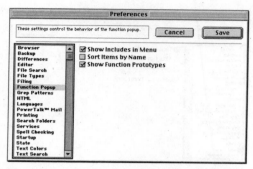

Figure B.8 The Function Popup Preferences window.

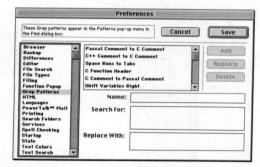

Figure B.9 The Grep Patterns window.

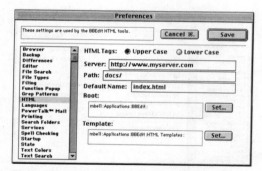

Figure B.10 The HTML Preferences window.

PREFERENCES

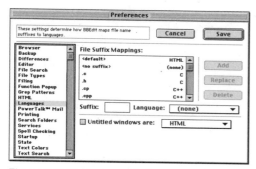

Figure B.11 The Languages Preferences window.

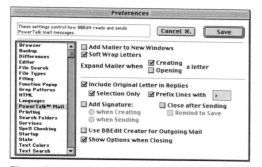

Figure B.12 The PowerTalk Mail Preferences window.

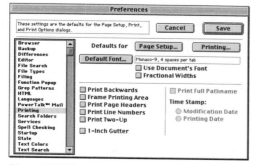

Figure B.13 The Printing Preferences window.

Languages (Figure B.11)

File Suffix Mappings—a list of the programming languages BBEdit understands.

Untitled Windows Are—when selected, will set the default language or style for untitled documents.

PowerTalk Mail (Figure B.12)

PowerTalk Mail preferences fall beyond the scope of this book.

Printing (Figure B.13)

Defaults for Page Setup—sets default Page Setup such as orientation and paper size.

Defaults for Printing—sets defaults for the printer.

Default Font—sets default printed text font (user can use document's screen default and set spacing by fractional widths).

Print Backwards—prints document in reverse order, last page first.

Frame Printing Area—surrounds the printing area with a double border.

Print Page Headers—prints a page header containing document name and time printed.

Print Line Numbers—prints line numbers by each line.

Print Two Up—prints two miniature document pages on one sheet of paper.

1-Inch Gutter—provides a one inch gutter at the left margin.

Print Full Pathname—prints the path of the document on each page.

Time Stamp—determines the time stamp, whether it is when the file was modified or when it was printed.

Search Folders (Figure B.14)

Use this preference box to add folders to the Find dialog box.

Services (Figure B.15)

BBEdit Plug-Ins—enables BBEdit Plug-In Tools under the Tool menu.

XTND Translation—when enabled, allows BBEdit to open a wide variety of files.

Internet Config—uses the Internet Config application to set Internet applications.

PowerTalk Mail—when selected, enables PowerTalk Mail.

Spell Checking (Figure B.16)

This preference indicates the location of BBEdit's built-in dictionary as well as any external dictionary that supports Apple Word Services.

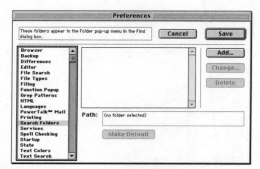

Figure B.14 The Search Folders Preferences window.

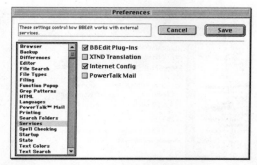

Figure B.15 The Services Preferences window.

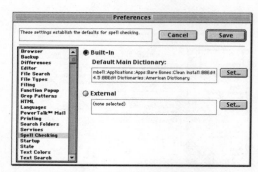

Figure B.16 The Spell Checking Preferences window.

PREFERENCES

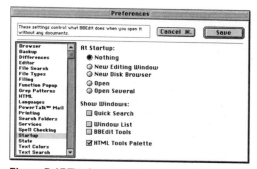

Figure B.17 The Startup Preferences window.

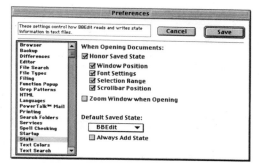

Figure B.18 The State Preferences window.

Startup (Figure B.17)

Nothing—when selected, does not open anything upon BBEdit launch.

New Editing Window—opens a new editing window when BBEdit is launched.

New Disk Browser—opens a disk browser window when BBEdit is launched.

Open—displays an Open dialog box when BBEdit is launched.

Open Several—opens the dialog box Open Several when BBEdit is launched.

Quick Search—opens the Quick Search dialog box when BBEdit is launched.

Window List—opens the floating Windows palette when BBEdit is launched.

BBEdit Tools—opens the Tools window when BBEdit is launched.

HTML Tools Palette—opens the HTML tools window when BBEdit is launched.

State (Figure B.18)

Honor Saved State—determines the condition of saved documents when opened in BBEdit including:

  Window Position—preserves the position of the window during saving.

  Font Settings—preserves font choice of the document when saved.

  Selection Range—stores a range of selected text when the document is saved.

  Scrollbar Position—preserves the position of the scrollbar during saving.

Zoom Window When Opening—opens window to full size, ignoring state information.

Default Saved State—selects the amount of state information saved with each file.

Always Add State—adds the state information from the default saved state to saved files.

Text Colors (Figure B.19)

Use Text Colors to determine the text color of programming and HTML language.

Text Search (Figure B.20)

Show Entire Dialog—when selected, shows all options available in the Find dialog box.

Entire Word—when selected, forces the search to match entire words in the search string.

Wrap Around—when selected, causes the search to continue through the document back to the insertion point.

Case Sensitive—when selected, forces the search to match case.

Grep—when selected, allows the use of grep patterns during searches.

Selection Only—when selected, conducts searches only in selected text.

Extend Selection—when selected, extends selection from the cursor to the end of the matched text string.

Find & Replace All—when all matches have been found and replaced, gives the user the option of either leaving windows open or saving all changes to disk.

Batch Find—after a multi-file search, displays the results in a browser window.

Search Nested Folders—during a multi-file search, searches folders nested within folders.

Skip ( ) Folders—during a multi-file search, skips folders surrounded by parentheses.

File Type—lets user limit the type of files searched during a multi-file search.

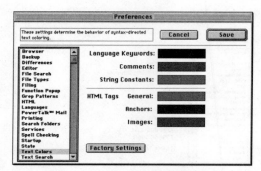

Figure B.19 The Text Colors Preferences window.

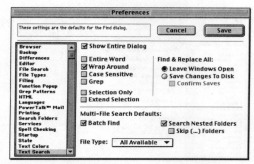

Figure B.20 The Text Search Preferences window.

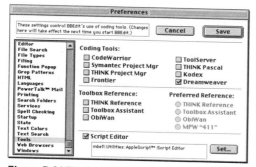

Figure B.21 The Tools Preferences window.

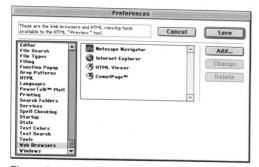

Figure B.22 The Web Browsers Preferences window.

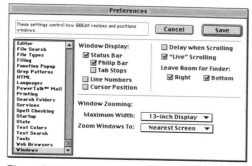

Figure B.23 The Windows Preferences window.

Tools (Figure B.21)

Sets preferences for a script editor, as well as coding tools, which is beyond the scope of this book.

Web Browsers (Figure B.22)

Lists the Web browsers recognized by BBEdit for use with the Preview feature. This list can be customized to include new browsers.

Windows (Figure B.23)

Status Bar—determines if a status bar will appear in a window and indicates whether a Philip bar and/or tab stops will be shown.

Line Numbers—lists a number beside each line in a document.

Cursor Position—indicates the exact position of the cursor in the document.

Delay When Scrolling—uses a slight delay when moving the scrolling bar.

"Live" Scrolling—moves the text in conjunction with the scrolling of the document.

Leave Room for Finder—leaves room at right and/or bottom of the screen for icons.

Maximum Width—sets the maximum window width.

Zoom Windows To:—used to specify which screen is used for zoomed windows.

PREFERENCES

Appendix C: Additional Tools

BBEdit performs the functions of a text-editing program wonderfully. There are several excellent companion programs, however, that you may want to add to your Web creator's toolbox.

Web Browsers

In HTML development, Web browsers are useful for their ability to preview HTML documents. The two predominant Web browsers are in fierce competition with each other for customer loyalty, constantly updating and improving their products.

- **Netscape Navigator**
  Netscape Navigator, written by the developers of the first Web browser, is now part of a suite of collaborative software, but at its heart it is still a Web browser. You can download Netscape Navigator from the Netscape homepage at http://home.netscape.com/.

- **Internet Explorer**
  Not the first Web browser to market, but Internet Explorer has all the resources of Microsoft behind it, which makes it a formidable competitor. You can download Internet Explorer from Microsoft's homepage at http://www.microsoft.com/.

FTP

Many users rely on FTP, or File Transfer
Protocol, to transfer files from their local
machines to remote servers, and vice versa.
Keep in mind that BBEdit has built-in FTP
capabilities.

■ **Fetch**
Fetch is the FTP program of choice for
most Macintosh users. It is free to educa-
tional users; otherwise, there is a small
shareware fee. Fetch can transfer files in
several formats and can delete files as well.
You can find out more about Fetch at
http://www.dartmouth.edu/pages/softdev/
fetch.html.

Image Editing

BBEdit can do many things, but it has
absolutely no image-editing functions
whatsoever. You must add a program
designed for editing graphics.

■ **Adobe Photoshop**
The granddaddy of image editing programs, Photoshop has the capability to
edit images and create original designs.
It can save files in several formats including GIF and JPEG (both required in Web
pages). You can find out more about
Photoshop at http://www.adobe.com/.

■ **GraphicConverter**
GraphicConverter has limited image-
editing capabilities, but it converts files
to even more formats than Adobe
Photoshop can—and it's economically
priced. It is a shareware program available
for download at most shareware sites,
including http://www.download.com/.

APPENDIX D:
SPECIAL CHARACTERS

The following information is from the HTML Resource Guide and is presented here with the permission of the authors, Jeremy Hall, Vince Shrader, and Jack Wilson.

Special Characters

CHARACTER	CODE	ENTITY NAME	CHARACTER	CODE	ENTITY NAME
"	&#34;	&quot;	°	&#176;	&deg;
&	&#38;	&amp;	±	&#177;	&plusmn;
<	&#60;	&lt;	2	&#178;	&sup2;
>	&#62;	&gt;	3	&#179;	&sup3;
(blank space)			´	&#180;	&acute;
¡	&#161;	&iexcl;	µ	&#181;	&micro;
¢	&#162;	&cent;	¶	&#182;	&para;
£	&#163;	&pound;	·	&#183;	&middot;
¤	&#164;	&curren;	¸	&#184;	&cedil;
¥	&#165;	&yen;	1	&#185;	&sup1;
¦	&#166;	&brvbar;	º	&#186;	&ordm;
		&brkbar;	»	&#187;	&raquo;
§	&#167;	&sect;	π	&#188;	&frac14;
¨	&#168;	&uml;	Π	&#189;	&frac12;
		&die;	≤	&#190;	&frac34;
©	&#169;	&copy;	¿	&#191;	&iquest;
ª	&#170;	&ordf;	À	&#192;	&Agrave;
«	&#171;	&laquo;	Á	&#193;	&Aacute;
	&#172;	&not;	Â	&#194;	&Acirc;
	&#173;	&shy;	Ã	&#195;	&Atilde;
®	&#174;	&reg;	Ä	&#196;	&Auml;
¯	&#175;	&macr;	Å	&#197;	&Aring;
		&hibar;	Æ	&#198;	&AElig;

Special Characters *(continued)*

CHARACTER	CODE	ENTITY NAME	CHARACTER	CODE	ENTITY NAME
Ç	&#199;	&Ccedil;	ã	&#227;	&atilde;
È	&#200;	&Egrave;	ä	&#228;	&auml;
É	&#201;	&Eacute;	å	&#229;	&aring;
Ê	&#202;	&Ecirc;	æ	&#230;	&aelig;
Ë	&#203;	&Euml;	ç	&#231;	&ccedil;
Ì	&#204;	&Igrave;	è	&#232;	&egrave;
Í	&#205;	&Iacute;	é	&#233;	&eacute;
Î	&#206;	&Icirc;	ê	&#234;	&ecirc;
Ï	&#207;	&Iuml;	ë	&#235;	&euml;
‹	&#208;	&ETH;	ì	&#236;	&igrave;
		&Dstrok;	í	&#237;	&iacute;
Ñ	&#209;	&Ntilde;	î	&#238;	&icirc;
Ò	&#210;	&Ograve;	ï	&#239;	&iuml;
Ó	&#211;	&Oacute;	›	&#240;	&eth;
Ô	&#212;	&Ocirc;	ñ	&#241;	&ntilde;
Õ	&#213;	&Otilde;	ò	&#242;	&ograve;
Ö	&#214;	&Ouml;	ó	&#243;	&oacute;
×	&#215;	&times;	ô	&#244;	&ocirc;
Ø	&#216;	&Oslash;	õ	&#245;	&otilde;
Ù	&#217;	&Ugrave;	ö	&#246;	&ouml;
Ú	&#218;	&Uacute;	÷	&#247;	&divide;
Û	&#219;	&Ucirc;	ø	&#248;	&oslash;
Ü	&#220;	&Uuml;	ù	&#249;	&ugrave;
†	&#221;	&Yacute;	ú	&#250;	&uacute;
fi	&#222;	&THORN;	û	&#251;	&ucirc;
ß	&#223;	&szlig;	ü	&#252;	&uuml;
à	&#224;	&agrave;	‡	&#253;	&yacute;
á	&#225;	&aacute;	fl	&#254;	&thorn;
â	&#226;	&acirc;	ÿ	&#255;	&yuml;

APPENDIX E: COLOR CHART

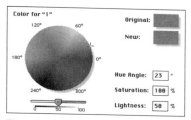

Figure E.1 The familiar Macintosh Color Picker.

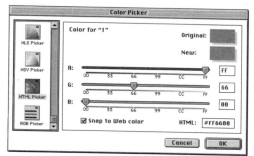

Figure E.2 Mac OS 8 includes built-in HTML color-picking abilities.

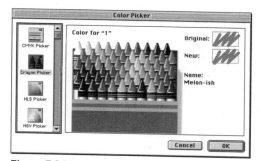

Figure E.3 How much easier can picking a color get?

The Hexadecimal Code

On the Mac OS, choosing colors has always been easy. The Color Picker (see **Figure E.1**) provides an intuitive interface, and it's even better under Mac OS 8, which lets you pick colors for use on the Web (see **Figure E.2**), and using a Crayon-style color chooser, as in **Figure E.3** (my personal favorite).

Although today's computers can display millions of colors, only 216 are actually considered "Web-safe" colors—that is, colors that display uniformly without dithering on any computer platform. BBEdit has a tool to help you choose Web-safe colors for your HTML documents (see **Figure E.4**).

On computer monitors, colors are made by mixing the primary colors are red, green, and blue. These colors can be indicated in an HTML document through the use of the hexadecimal system of color codes.

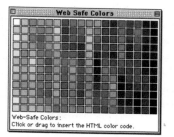

Figure E.4 BBEdit's Web Color Palette tool.

Hexadecimal codes are made up of six digits—the numbers 0 through 9 and the letters A through F—in three pairs, one for each component color (see **Figure E.5**). The code 000000 indicates black, and the code FFFFFF indicates white. All other colors fit in between. For example, FF0000 indicates the presence of red and the absence of green and blue, thus presenting the color red. The code 00FF00 wuld indicates green, and the code 0000FF blue.

Figure E.5 The key to understanding hexadecimal color codes starts with the six digits that comprise the codes.

Frequently Used Colors

Table E.1 is a list of the most frequently used colors and those colors that have been given names.

URL References

Several Web pages provide hexadecimal codes for various colors, as well as information on how to effectively use color in your Web document. You can also locate color palettes that will work with popular graphic programs to guarantee that your color choices will be viewed effectively on most monitors.

Visit these URLs for more information on creating browser-safe HTML document.

http://www.infi.net/wwwimages/colorindex.html

http://www.lynda.com

http://www.Webmotion.com/Websurfshop/ Colorcode

http://www.neosoft.com/~pphset/rbb/ favorite.htm

http://silk.Webware.co.nz/ColorCalculator

You can locate many others by using your favorite Web search engine and entering the word "hexadecimal," or by visiting Yahoo at the following URL:

http://www.yahoo.com/Computers_and_ Internet/Internet/World_Wide_Web/ Page_Design_and_Layout/Color_Information

COLOR CHART

Table E.1

Frequently Used Colors

NAME	HEXADECIMAL EQUIVALENT	NAME	HEXADECIMAL EQUIVALENT	NAME	HEXADECIMAL EQUIVALENT
Aquamarine	70DB93	Goldenrod	DBDB70	Old Gold	CFB53B
Baker's Chocolate	5C3317	Green	00FF00	Orange	FF7F00
Black	000000	Green Copper	527F76	Orange Red	FF2400
Blue	0000FF	Green Yellow	93DB70	Orchid	DB70DB
Blue Violet	9F5F9F	Grey	C0C0C0	Pale Green	8FBC8F
Brass	B5A642	Hunter Green	215E21	Pink	BC8F8F
Bright Gold	D9D919	Indian Red	4E2F2F	Plum	EAADEA
Bronze	8C7853	Khaki	9F9F5F	Quartz	D9D9F3
Bronze II	A67D3D	Light Blue	C0D9D9	Red	FF0000
Brown	A62A2A	Light Grey	A8A8A8	Rich Blue	5959AB
Cadet Blue	5F9F9F	Light Steel Blue	8F8FBD	Salmon	6F4242
Cool Copper	D98719	Light Wood	E9C2A6	Scarlet	8C1717
Copper	B87333	Lime Green	32CD32	Sea Green	238E68
Coral	FF7F00	Magenta	FF00FF	Semi-Sweet Chocolate	6B4226
Cornflower Blue	42426F	Mandarin Orange	E47833	Sienna	8E6B23
Cyan	00FFFF	Maroon	8E236B	Silver	E6E8FA
Dark Brown	5C4033	Medium Aquamarine	32CD99	Sky Blue	3299CC
Dark Green	2F4F2F	Medium Blue	3232CD	Slate Blue	007FFF
Dark Green Copper	4A766E	Medium Forest Green	6B8E23	Spicy Pink	FF1CAE
Dark Olive Green	4F4F2F	Medium Goldenrod	EAEAAE	Spring Green	00FF7F
Dark Orchid	9932CD	Medium Orchid	9370DB	Steel Blue	236B8E
Dark Purple	871F78	Medium Sea Green	426F42	Summer Sky	38B0DE
Dark Slate Blue	6B238E	Medium Slate Blue	7F00FF	Tan	DB9370
Dark Slate Grey	2F4F4F	Medium Spring Green	7FFF00	Thistle	D8BFD8
Dark Tan	97694F	Medium Turquoise	70DBDB	Turquoise	ADEAEA
Dark Turquoise	7093DB	Medium Violet Red	DB7093	Very Dark Brown	5C4033
Dark Wood	855E42	Medium Wood	A68064	Very Light Grey	CDCDCD
Dim Grey	545454	Midnight Blue	2F2F4F	Violet	4F2F4F
Dusty Rose	856363	Navy Blue	23238E	Violet Red	CC3299
Feldspar	D19275	Neon Blue	4D4DFF	Wheat	D8D8BF
Firebrick	8E2323	Neon Pink	FF6EC7	White	FFFFFF
Forest Green	238E23	New Midnight Blue	00009C	Yellow	FFFF00
Gold	CD7F32	New Tan	EBC79E	Yellow Green	99CC32

COLOR CHART

APPENDIX F:
HTML RESOURCE GUIDE

The following information is from the HTML Resource Guide and is presented here with the permission of the authors, Jeremy Hall, Vince Shrader, and Jack Wilson.

Introduction

Have you been searching for a good quick reference guide for HTML? Search no longer, you have arrived! And now the new and improved version 1.1!

When I was beginning to learn a bit about HTML, I always wondered why I could not find a straight forward list of tags and what they did. The books always seemed to go to long and the online stuff always seemed to be hard to follow. So, I decided to put something together that fills that niche. Yes, it does contain a mixture of tags from different levels of HTML standards and not necessarily all the tags that have been introduced. I'll leave it up to you to decide which you will and will not use according to your personal preferences. There are many new improvements to this version of the guide, so be sure to see the version history in the "Contact Us" section for those updates!

This is a document that you can contribute to. If you see any part that could use some correction, improvement or otherwise needs help, please contact me using the information included in this document. I am sure their are mistakes, so if you could help me out by finding them and letting me know, that would be a big help! If I ever find the time, there will also be an HTML primer available much like this guide.

How to Use This Guide

This guide is an export of the online version available at the following URL:

http://www.qi3.com/hall/html/

The same document is available in a DocMaker format, located on the Web site, which includes:

- Table of Contents will jump you to the different subject areas.
- Search will find each occurrence (in order) of any text you input
- Quick List is a straight list of HTML tags with buttons which jump you to the applicable description.
- Description is a (hopefully concise) explanation of HTML tags.
- Examples shows how the HTML tags would be laid out in code format.
- On The Web are buttons on the Examples page that jump you straight into your browser to see how the tag actually looks when put into use. **See note below.
- Special Characters new to version 1.1! ISO characters and their equivalents.

Be sure to use the Search capability, this makes the guide a great resource while you are writing your HTML. Just click the button and then enter the tag you are looking for. Click 'OK' several times to jump straight through to the description and examples.

In this version of the guide, you'll find the following sections, all of which correspond to the DocMaker and HTML versions:

- Introduction
- How to Use this Guide
- A Quick HTML List
- Description of Tags
- Additional Resources
- Contact the Authors
- Licensing Information
- Shameless Plug
- Version History

The only section not included in this guide is a collection of examples, which you can find in the other versions. The following abbreviations are used in all the version of the HTML Resource Guide to indicate browser compatibility :

- (NS) Netscape Navigator
- (IE) Internet Explorer
- (NS/IE) Netscape Navigator and Internet Explorer

A Quick HTML List

The following section lists the HTML tags that are described in more detail in the following section. Please see the DocMaker version of this guide for hyperlinks to online examples of these tags.

General

```
<HTML>...</HTML>
<HEAD>...</HEAD>
<TITLE>...</TITLE>
<BODY>...</BODY>
<!DOCTYPE>
```

Formatting

```
<B>...</B>
<I>...</I>
<U>...</U>
<S>...</S> OR <STRIKE>...</STRIKE>
<TT></TT>
<BLINK></BLINK>
<BASEFONT SIZE=x>
<FONT></FONT>
<Hx></Hx>
<CITE></CITE>
<CODE></CODE>
<DFN></DFN>
<EM></EM>
<KBD></KBD>
<XMP></XMP>
<PRE></PRE>
<STRONG></STRONG>
<SAMP></SAMP>
<VAR></VAR>
<ADDRESS></ADDRESS>
<SMALL>
<BIG>
<SUB>
<SUP>
```

Alignment

```
<Hx ALIGN=y></Hx>
<P ALIGN=x></P>
<BLOCKQUOTE></BLOCKQUOTE>
<CENTER></CENTER>
```

Links & Images

```
<A HREF="document.html"></A>
<A HREF="#target"></A>
<A NAME="target"></A>
<IMG SRC="image.gif" ALIGN=x>
<MAP>...</MAP>
```

Dividers

`<BR>`

`<P>`

`<HR SIZE=X WIDTH=Y>`

`<NOBR></NOBR>`

`<WBR>`

Lists

`<OL>...</OL>`

`<UL>...</UL>`

`<DL>...</DL>` including `<DT>` and `<DL>`

`<DIR>...</DIR>`

`<MENU>...</MENU>`

`<LI>`

`<DT>`

`<DD>`

Tables & Columns

`<TABLE>...</TABLE>`

`<CAPTION ALIGN=x>...</CAPTION>`

`<TR>...</TR>`

`<TH>...</TH>`

`<TD>...</TD>`

`<MULTICOL>` or `<COLGROUP>`

Forms

`<FORM ACTION="action URL"`
→ `METHOD=GET/POST>...</FORM>`

`<INPUT NAME="name" VALUE="value" TYPE=x`
→ `SIZE=y MAXLENGTH=z>`

`<TEXTAREA NAME="name" ROWS=x`
→ `COLS=y>...</TEXTAREA>`

Miscellaneous

`<FRAMESET>...</FRAMESET>` (All frames tags & modifiers)

`<!-- -->`

`<META>`

`<SPACER>`

`<MARQUEE>`

`<EMBED>`

`<OBJECT>`

Description of Tags

The following section describes the HTML tags mentioned above in brief detail. Please see the DocMaker version of this guide for hyperlinks to online examples of these tags.

General

`<HTML>...</HTML>`

The purpose of the HTML tag is to tell the web browsing software that the document it's looking at is indeed an HTML page. Be sure to place `<HTML>` at the top of every HTML page you create. Similarly, place a `</HTML>` tag at the bottom of every document.

`<HEAD>...</HEAD>`

The head tag is used to tell the browser what part of the document is the top section, or the head. This section holds the title, meta and can also the JavaScript information.

`<TITLE>...</TITLE>`

The title contains the text that appears in the title bar of your browser window. This is located within the `<HEAD>` container.

`<BODY>...</BODY>`

The largest part of your HTML document is the body, which contains the content of your document (shown within the display area of your browser window).

Attributes: (on all the following, the default colors will be used if omitted)

text - used to set the base color for the normal text within the document

link - used to set a specific color for text links

alink - used to set a specific color for an active link

vlink - used to set a specific color for a visited link

bgcolor - used to set a specific background color (all the color attributes are best if set equal to a hexadecimal number equivalent)

background - used to specify a graphic file to tiled for the background. If a bgcolor is also set, the page will appear in that color until the background graphic is loaded.

bgsound - used to load and play a sound file in the background, also requires the sound to be EMBEDDED if Netscape. (NS3/IE)2

bgproperties - when set to fixed, locks the background image into place as a water-mark.(IE)

leftmargin/topmargin - defines size of margins in pixels. (IE)

<!DOCTYPE> Document Type Declaration

Specifies the version of HTML used in the document. !DOCTYPE is the first element in any HTML document. !DOCTYPE is a required element for any HTML 3.2-compliant document.

Formatting

<B>...</B> Bold

Used to bold text. Often this reproduces the same effect as the strong emphasis tag.

<I>...</I> Italics

Used to italicize text.

<U>...</U> Underline

Used to underline text; not widely supported as underlining typically is associated with links, though NS3 began supporting it.

<S>...</S> or
<STRIKE>...</STRIKE> Strikeout

Displays the text with a line through the middle, striking it out.

<TT>...</TT> Typewriter Text

Used for typewriter text, a fixed-width font supposedly like a typewriter.

<BLINK>...</BLINK> Blinking Text (NS/IE)

A somewhat annoying option when overused, all the text that appears between these tags will blink incessantly.

<BASEFONT SIZE=x> Base Font Size

Allows you to set the font size of your entire document to be a specified size in relation to what the user has set in their browser. The 'x' would be a number between 1 and 7.

<FONT>...</FONT> Font Modification (NS/IE)

The font tag makes it possible to make temporary changes in text attributes within the body of your document. A big advantage to this tag is that changes can be made mid-sentence, not forcing a new line break like the heading tag.

Attributes:

size - used to change the size of the text. The size can be set as an absolute value or proportional, i.e. '+' or '-' a certain number. These numbers are between 1 and 7.

color - a newer attribute that (in some browsers) allows you to change the test color. This is a hexadecimal number or there are also a few names that can be used, i.e. red, blue, green, etc. This option will be ignored by non-capable browsers.

face - Sets the font. A list of font names can be specified. If the first font is available on the system, it will be used; otherwise, the second will be tried, and so on. If none are available, a default font will be used. (NS3/IE)3

<Hx>...</Hx> Heading

HTML has six levels of headings. The symbol 'x' equals, numbers 1 through 6, with 1 being the most prominent. Headings are displayed in larger and/or bolder fonts than normal body text. The first heading in each document should ideally be tagged <H1>.

Attributes:

align - used to align the heading text either left, right or center.

<CITE>...</CITE> Citation

Used for titles of books, films, etc. Typically displayed in italics.

<CODE>...</CODE> Code

Used for computer code. Displayed in a fixed-width font.

<DFN>...</DFN> Definition

Used for emphasizing a definition. No recognizable change in most browsers.

<EM>...</EM> Emphasis

Used for emphasis. Typically displayed in italics.

<KBD>...</KBD> Keyboard Entry

Used for user keyboard entry. Typically displayed in plain fixed-width font.

<XMP>...</XMP> Preformatted - No tags

Preformatted without tags. Handy for showing HTML tags on screen if you are explaining how tags work.

<PRE>...</PRE> Preformatted

The <PRE> tag (which stands for "preformatted") generates text in a fixed-width font. This tag also makes spaces, new lines, and tabs significant (multiple spaces are displayed as multiple spaces, and lines break in the same locations as in the source HTML file). This is useful for program listings, among other things.

<STRONG>...</STRONG> Strong Emphasis

Used for strong emphasis. Typically displayed in bold.

<SAMP>...</SAMP>

Used for a sequence of literal characters. Displayed in a fixed-width font.

<VAR>...</VAR> Variable

Used for a variable, where you will replace the variable with specific information. Typically displayed in italics.

<ADDRESS>...</ADDRESS> Address

The <ADDRESS> tag is generally used to specify the author of a document, a way to contact the author (e.g., an email address), and a revision date. It is usually the last item in a file.

<SMALL>...</SMALL> Small Text (NS/IE)

A bit of an obvious tag. The text enclosed within this container will appear smaller in relation to the surrounding text. Basically the same effect as reducing the font size by −1.

<BIG>...</BIG> Big Text (NS/IE)

A bit of an obvious tag again.. The text enclosed within this container will appear bigger in relation to the surrounding text. Basically the same effect as reducing the font size by +1.

_{...} Subscript (NS/IE)

The text enclosed within this container will appear as a subscript. This is very useful for creating the footnotes or endnotes or doing mathematical formulas. The text will be one font size smaller and half a line below the rest of the text.

^{...} Superscript (NS/IE)

The text enclosed within this container will appear as a superscript. This is very useful for creating the footnotes or endnotes or doing mathematical formulas. The text will be one font size smaller and half a line above the rest of the text.

Alignment Tags

<Hx ALIGN=y></Hx> See previous entry

<P ALIGN=y></P> See entry below

<BLOCKQUOTE>...</BLOCKQUOTE> Block Quotation

Use the <BLOCKQUOTE> tag to include lengthy quotations in a separate block on the screen. Most browsers generally indent from both margins for the quotation to offset it from surrounding text.

<CENTER>...</CENTER> Center

Allows you to center text and even objects on your screen.

Links & Images

<A>...</A> Anchor

The anchor tag gives interactivity to an HTML document. This allows you to create links to other Internet pages, documents and downloadable files. Anything that appears between the begin and end anchor tags will take you to the specified destination when clicked.

Attributes:

href - the basic attribute to an anchor tag which tells the destination of the link. This can specify a link within the current document or outside document or file. Outside links can be absolute (include the full URL including http, mailto etc.) or relative (within the same folder or directory on the WWW server).

mailto - used within a href reference to create a hyperlink for emailing.

name - used for specifying the location and name of an internal link.

target - if using frames, this specifies what frame or window to load the link into. See the entry under frames below.

<IMG> Image

To include an image in a web document, you need to use an image tag. Make certain the file name ends with ".gif" or .jpg" for GIF or JPEG images. By default, the bottom of an image is aligned with the text. There are numerous attributes for the image tag.

Attributes:

src - the basic and necessary element of an image tag which specifies the location of the image file to be displayed.

width - specifies the width of the image. Optional, but recommended for faster layout of your page. This can be used to stretch or shrink the display of the image.

height - specifies the height of the image. Same description as width.

border - specifies a border with (in pixels) when an image is used as a hyperlink. Set the border width to zero if you want no border to appear. (It is good etiquette to also include a text version of the link as well.)

align - align the image to the left, right, middle, bottom, top, and others that are not as widely supported. When defining the alignment, the image appears where specified and the text wraps to the other side.

alt - gives an optional text to appear if the person is not loading images or using a non-graphical browser.

lowsrc - an optional image to load first and faster to give a feel for the page before the larger image loads. If using this feature, be sure the lowsrc is much smaller!

usemap - if using a client-side image map, this specifies what coding to refer to.

<MAP>...</MAP> Client-Side Image Map NS2/IE2

A new and very cool feature that allows the use of a graphic as an image map without the use of server image maps. There are several modifications that need to be made for this tag to work. First you must find the coordinates around the sections to be clickable. Then set up the code to work according to those clickable points. You must also include the USEMAP attribute in the image tag.

Attributes:

name - essential attribute giving the code a name to be referenced by for the image tag.

usemap - included with the image tag to specify what coding to refer to.

<AREA> Client-Side Image Map (cont'd) (NS2/IE3)

Part of the <MAP> tag; much like the <LI> is to a list. It is with this tag that you specify the different areas that are clickable and where they go.

Attributes:

shape - determines the shape of the clickable area being defined; can be rectangle (rect), polygon (poly), circles (circle), and default (default). Default defines an action those parts of the image that do not have a shape given.

coords - sets the coordinates of the area. For a rectangle and they are given as "left, top, right, bottom" and a circle is a defined as a center point and then a radius (a total of three numbers).

href - same as when in an anchor tag, specifies the action when the area is clicked.

nohref - specifies an area to be non-clickable, or have no action associated with it.

target - if using frames, this specifies what frame or window to load the link into. See the entry under frames below.

Dividers

 Line Break

The <BR> tag forces a line break with no extra (white) space between lines.

Attributes:

clear - used to discontinue wrapping next to an inline graphic and continue one line below the graphic. Can be set equal to left, right and center.

<P>...</P> Paragraph

Creates a line break and starts a new paragraph. Without <P> tags, the document becomes one large paragraph. The </P> closing tag can be omitted. This is because browsers understand that when they encounter a <P> tag, it implies that there is an end to the previous paragraph.

Attributes:

align - for aligning text; can be set equal to left, center or right

<HR> Horizontal Rule

The <HR> tag produces a horizontal line the width of the browser window. It's often used as a way to break up information in your document. The WIDTH and SIZE attributes may be used with <HR> individually or together.

Attributes:

noshade - forces the line to be solid rather than shadowed or 3-D (NS/IE)

width=x - Designates the width of the rule with 'x' equaling the rule's percentage (or absolute pixel width) to the size of the browser window. (NS/IE)

size=x - Designates the thickness of the rule with 'x' equaling the number of pixels.

align - aligns the line to the left, center or right (NS/IE)

<NOBR>...</NOBR> No (Line) Break (NS/IE)

No break allows you to force text to stay on the same line, much like the PRE tag, but does not start on a new line at the beginning of the tag or force the text to a fixed font. Good for poetry that just must look a certain way.

<WBR> Word Break (NS/IE)

Used inside of the NOBR tag to specify breaking points, or when to start a new line.

Lists

<OL> Ordered List

A numbered list (also called an ordered list, from which the tag name derives) is identical to an unnumbered list, except it uses <OL> instead of <UL>. The items are tagged using the same <LI> tag. These lists can be nested to form an outline format, automatically assigning different numbering formats for the nested lists.

Attributes:

type - allows for specification of numbering type; can be set to disc, square or circle

<UL>...</UL> Unnumbered (unorganized) List

Makes an unnumbered, bulleted list. Each item in the list appears between the UL tags, and is preceded by an <LI> tag. These lists can be nested to form an outline format, automatically assigning different symbols for the nested lists.

Attributes:

type - allows for specification of bullet type; can be set to disc, square or circle

<DL>...</DL> Definition List

A definition list usually consists of alternating a definition term (coded as <DT>) and a definition (coded as <DD>). Web browsers generally format the definition on a new line and typically indented.

<DIR>...</DIR> Directory List

Not used very much anymore, but acts the same as an unnumbered list. Can be used to help you keep you coding organized.

<MENU>...</MENU> Menu List

Not used very much anymore, but acts the same as an unnumbered list. Can be used to help you keep you coding organized.

<LI> List Item

The <LI> (list item) tag is followed by the individual item. Each item in a numbered or unnumbered list is preceded by an <LI> tag. The closing </LI> tag is optional, but not needed.

<DT> Definition Term

Used within a definition list (<DL>) to specify the term or stem of the list item. Starts on a new line of text.

<DD> Definition Data

Used within a definition list (<DL>) to specify the definition or body of the list item. Usually appears on the following line of text and indented from the left margin.

Tables

<TABLE> ... </TABLE> Table

Defines a table in HTML. Tables are very useful for controlling the layout of a page so that it appears exactly as intended. Tables were introduced by Netscape, but are now widely supported enough that I will not designate it as limited only to the big two browsers.

Attributes:

border - to specify a visible border width for a table. A border of 1 pixel width is the default if you do not specify the width. Use BORDER=0 if you do not want to show a border.

cellspacing - specify a pixel width for spacing between cells, visible if a border > 1.

cellpadding - specify a pixel width/value for spacing from the cell border and the contents of the cell.

width - give pixel dimensions or percentage for the width of the entire table.

bordercolor - specifies a color for the table border (hex, rgb, name). (IE)

bordercolorlight - specifies a light color for the 3-D table border (hex, rgb, name). (IE)

bordercolordark - specifies a dark color for the 3-D table border (hex, rgb, name). (IE)

<CAPTION> ...</CAPTION> Table Caption

Defines the caption for the title of the table. The default position of the title is centered at the top of the table. NOTE: Any kind of markup tag can be used in the caption.

Attributes:

align - specify whether the caption appears at the top or bottom of the table

<TR> ... </TR> Table Row

Specifies a table row within a table. A table cells and headings will be contained within a table row.

Attributes:

align - specify default alignment for the entire row of cells, including left, right, center.

valign - default vertical alignment for the entire row, including top, bottom, middle.

<TH> ... </TH> Table Heading

Defines a table header cell. By default the text in this cell is bold and centered. Table header cells may contain other attributes to determine the characteristics of the cell and/or its contents. See Table Attributes below for more information.

Attributes:

align - specify default alignment for the contents of the cell, including left, right, center.

valign - vertical alignment for the contents of the cell, including top, bottom, middle.

width/height - dimensions for the cell; may be in pixel value or percentage of the table.

colspan - specify how many columns for the current cell to span or cross.

rowspan - specify how many rows for the current cell to span or cross.

bgcolor - set the background color for the table cell. (NS3/IE)

<TD> ... </TD> Table Data (cell)

Defines a table data cell. By default the text in this cell is aligned left and centered vertically. Table data cells may contain other attributes to determine the characteristics of the cell and/or its contents. See Table Attributes below for more information.

Attributes:

align - specify default alignment for the contents of the cell, including left, right, center.

valign - vertical alignment for the contents of the cell, including top, bottom, middle.

width/height - dimensions for the cell; may be in pixel value or percentage of the table.

colspan - specify how many columns for the current cell to span or cross.

rowspan - specify how many rows for the current cell to span or cross.

bgcolor - set the background color for the table cell. (NS3/IE)

<MULTICOL> ... </MULTICOL> Multiple Columns NS

The MULTICOL tag is a container, and all the HTML between the starting and ending tag will be displayed in a multicolumn format. The tag can be nested. (IE) uses a format much different within tables which I will explore more and include in a later version of this guide.

Attributes:

cols - mandatory and controls how many columns the display will be split into. Layout will attempt to flow elements evenly across the columns to make each column about the same height. Unless the WIDTH attribute is specified, column width is adjusted to fill the available view.

gutter - the GUTTER attribute controls the amount of space between columns. It defaults to a value of 10 pixels.

width - specifies the width of an individual column in pixels.

Forms

<FORM>...</FORM> Form

The basic element of the form is the <FORM> tag. This begins and closes the area enclosing the form elements. Any HTML coding can be contained within the form area to enhance the look of your form. There are attributes within the form tag that are required to tell your browser where to send the information and how to do it.

Attributes:

action - tells your browser what URL to send the information to; this is typically a CGI program of some kind.

method - there are two options, 'get' or 'post'. The difference is actually somewhat complicated, but in simple language get encodes all the information into the URL that is sent and post sends the data separately from the actual call to the script. Which do you use? Typically you will be using a set program someone else has created, and they will tell you which one to use. Whew!

<INPUT> Input (Variables)

Input is the most common element within the form area. This allows you to specify text input fields, radio buttons, check boxes, selection lists and perhaps more as it is developed.

Attributes:

name - specifies the field or variable name; must be included.

value - specifies the default value for the variable when sent to the CGI program. This can also be specified as "hidden" to send information that you do not want the user seeing. This text appears within the field and can be deleted and/or replaced by the user.

type - this is where you specify what type input you are looking for, either text, radio, checkboxes, or selection menus. Be sure to see the coding examples for how to use these options.

size - when using a text input field, this tells how long it is (width in character's).

maxlength - when using a text input field, specifies how many characters the user is limited to for their input.

selected - when using a radio field, determines which button is selected by default (be sure to only select one!)

checked - when using a checkbox field, specifies which box(es) are selected.

<TEXTAREA>...</TEXTAREA> Form Text Area

When you are asking a user to input a large amount of text, use the text area element instead of a small one line text input box. You can assign the dimensions of the text area to help determine how much the user types. Text entered between the opening and closing tags will appear within the text area and can be deleted and/or replaced by the user.

Attributes:

name - specifies the field or variable name; must be included.

value - specifies the default value for the variable when sent to the CGI program.

rows - determines how long the text area will be (length in text lines).

cols - determines how wide the text area will be (width in characters).

wrap - specifies how you would like the text to wrap within the text area, usually 'virtual' if you do anything, but optional.

Miscellaneous

Frames (NS2/IE3)

You may wonder why frames was not put in a section of its own, like tables or lists. Although popular, frames are memory & bandwidth intensive, and usually not utilized very well. They are new enough that you should take care when using them and always offer a noframe alternative. Even though I may be a little biased against them, there are good uses for frames, and therefore let's get on to explaining them!

<FRAMESET>...</FRAMESET> Frame Container (NS2/IE3)

This is the main container for a frame. When creating a frame "defining" page, you leave out the BODY tag and use this tag for each frame. These can be nested to create frames within frames, much like a table. Frameset would be comparable to rows or columns in a table.

Attributes:

rows - a value that assign how much of the screen each row is allotted, given in fixed pixels, percentage number or '*' meaning take up the remaining space.

cols - follows same format as rows, only assigns the screen sections horizontally.

bordercolor - used to set a default color for the border of the frames. See the explanation below for conflicting situations. NS

<FRAME> Individual Frame (NS2/IE3)

This tag defines a single frame in a frameset. It is not a container so it has no matching end tag.

Attributes:

src - defines the source URL to be displayed in the frame. If omitted a blank space is displayed in the size of the frame.

name - defines a name for the window. Although this is not displayed, it is useful for targeting particular windows with links.

marginwidth - gives control of the margin width within a frame, defined in pixels.

marginheight - gives control of the margin height within a frame, defined in pixels.

scrolling - determines whether the frame contains a scroll bar, defined as "yes, no or auto". Be sure to include if your page may not fit within the frame display area.

noresize - specifies that the user cannot change the size of the frame. There is no value associated with the tag, it's inclusion only. This is optional and all frames are resizable by default.

frameborder - specifies the presence of a 3-D border for the frame. NS uses the options of yes or no, (IE) uses the options of 1 or 0.

bordercolor - used to set a specific color for the frame border. This can run into difficulties when two frames have conflicting border colors. Netscape defines the solution: "The attribute in the outer FRAMESET has the lowest priority. This in turn is overridden by the attribute used in a nested FRAMESET tag. Finally, the BORDERCOLOR attribute used in a FRAME tag overrides all previous FRAMESET tags"

<NOFRAMES>...</NOFRAMES> No Frame Option (NS2/IE3) (but for other browsers)

Option included on the primary frame document that provides information or alternate page layout for non-frames capable browsers. This is necessity if you are interested in reaching large portions of the web that choose not to use frames capable browsers.

TARGET - Targeting Links Within Frames (NS2/IE3)

This is an option for pointing your links into specific frames. These targets can be contained within the anchor tag, area tag of a client-side image map or within the base tag for an overall default destination. TIP: Before using frames, be sure you understand how to target links and how to make a link fill the whole window when it leaves your site.

Values: (set target equal to these within the anchor tag)

"window name" - set the target equal to the name of the window to load into.

"_blank" - will cause the link to always be loaded in a new blank window.

"_self" - causes the link to always load in the same window the anchor was clicked in.

"_parent" - makes the link load in the immediate FRAMESET parent of this document. This defaults to acting like "_self" if the document has no parent.

"_top" - makes the link load in the full body of the window. This is how you get out of your frames when leaving your site!

Other

<!-- --> Comments

Allows you to place comments within the code of your HTML document that does not appear when loaded up into a browser. This is handy for placing markers or reminders to yourself in a highly changing document.

<META> Meta Indexing

Embedding information for the server. Used for several options, especially for passing indexing information to search engines (both internal and the larger popular ones) and for automatic reloading or reloading to a different URL of your page (client-pull).

Attributes:

http-equiv - set this equal to a URL and time to be reloaded

name - name of the document/HTML file or descriptor for a search engine (such as description, keywords or author).

content - a short description of the content of the page

<SPACER> Invisible Spacer NS3

The new SPACER tag has the ability to enhance page formatting. A simple use of the tag would be to indent a paragraph. The SPACER tag can be used much like an image, with height, width and align attributes.

Attributes:

type - can be horizontal, vertical and block

width - specifies the width of the invisible space to be blocked off

height - specifies the height of the invisible space to be blocked off

align - align the invisible space much like an image, most used as left or right.

<MARQUEE> Scrolling Marquee (IE)

Creates a scrolling text marquee. This is only supported by Internet Explorer, though a popular Java applet has been widely used making it available for Netscape. Use this with care, it can become as annoying as the BLINK tag has become!

Attributes:

align - specifies how the surrounding text should align with the marquee. The align-type can be top, middle or bottom.

behavior - specifies how the text should behave. The possible values are:

scroll - start completely off one side, scroll all the way across and completely off, and then start again. This is the default.

slide - start completely off one side, scroll in, and stop as soon as the text touches the other margin

alternate - bounce back and forth within the marquee.

bgcolor - used to set a specific background color (all the color attributes are best if set equal to a hexadecimal number equivalent

direction - Specifies in which direction the text should scroll. The direction can be LEFT or RIGHT. The default is LEFT, which means scrolling to the left from the right

height/width - specifies the height and width of the marquee, either in pixels or as a percentage of the screen (a % sign is required in this case).

hspace/vspace - specifies the horizontal and vertical margin or buffer around the marquee

loop - specifies how many times the marquee message will loop. This can be a whole integer or INFINITE.

scrollamount - specifies the number of pixels between each successive draw of the marquee text.

scrolldelay - specifies the number of milliseconds between each successive draw of the marquee text.

<EMBED> Embeds an Object (NS/IE)

Indicates an embedded object. OBJECT is the preferred element for inserting objects for (IE), but EMBED is also supported by (IE). The OBJECT attributes are very similar, but also add several other options for specific types of objects.

Attributes:

src - location of the object data, just like any other link or image.

height/width - the height or width of the object specified in pixels.

name - the name used by other objects or elements to refer to this object.

palette - sets the color palette to the foreground or background color.

autostart - if playing a sound, this determines if it starts automatically (true/false).

loop - if a sound file, designates the number of times to loop.

Additional Resources
Hexadecimal Color Codes

Figuring out the correct hexadecimal equivalent for colors can be a real pain. Jack Wilson is a co-worker and friend of mine and has taken the time to make a color chart to use with this guide. There are two formats that you can use.

The first is created using table cells and bgcolor information, which requires that you have either (IE) 2+ or NS3 to view it. This file is packaged within the HTML Guide folder, and is available on the Web as well at:

http://www.qi3.com/hall/html/hexchart.html

The second is basically a screen capture of this chart, but can be viewed with any graphics program that supports JPEG format. This is a large file, so I chose not to include it within the basic HTML Guide folder, but it can also be downloaded separately from the download page at:

http://www.qi3.com/hall/html/images/
→ hexchart.jpg

Contact Information

As mentioned before, I would be happy to hear about any improvements that could be made to this document. I know that not all the latest and greatest "proposed" tags are in this document either. If you think a tag should be included or better explained, let me know. Also, if you would like to see a primer included or as a separate stand-alone document, let me know as well. I really would like to see this be a useful guide. Big thanks go to Vince Shrader as the primary co-author and editor of this document. Thanks to Jack Wilson for creating the Hex Color

Chart and his constant help throughout. Also, thanks to all those who emailed in your suggestions...keep 'em coming!

Thanks for all your comments to help make this a great resource for Macintosh HTML users.

Jeremy Hall

email: hallj@ed.byu.edu
home page: http://www.qi3.com/hall

Vince Shrader

email: shraderv@ed.byu.edu
home page: http://www.qi3.com/vince

Jack Wilson

email: wilsonj@ed.byu.edu (Hex Color Chart)

Snail Address:
205 MCKB
BYU
Provo, UT 84604

Licensing Information

This document is "emailware," "postcard-ware," and "helpmeware." First off, send either of us an email to let us know if this was helpful in any way. Second, if you are feeling kind, send us a postcard. Lastly and most important, please email us any suggestions to improve the functionality and content of this document! Of course, if feel extremely kind, I would never refuse monetary donations!

Shameless Plug

I (Jeremy) do web page design and would be more than happy to develop your page or web site. I do both graphical design and page layout, providing professional quality for a reasonable price. Contact me via email for a quote that will meet your needs and available resources.

Version History

Version 1.1

- Added Netscape (NS) and Internet Explorer (IE) indicators. On some the version number is included showing when the tag began to be supported.
- Added new tags not as widely supported or recently released.
- Added chapter on special (ISO) characters in response to many requests.
- Fixed several typos and some explanations

Version 1.0

- Initial public release, much more response and use than expected! A pleasant surprise!

APPENDIX G: GETTING HELP

Figure G.1 The first place to look for help.

Figure G.2 Balloon Help for BBEdit is very well implemented.

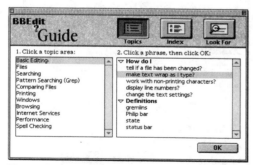

Figure G.3 The BBEdit Guide has answers to most questions.

There are numerous ways to obtain additional help and information about BBEdit. Several excellent resources for help, online and in print, are included in the commercial version of BBEdit. You can find more resources in bookstores and on the Web. To get started, take a look in the Help menu (see **Figure G.1**).

Balloon Help

One of the fastest and best resources for help, Balloon Help is just a menu click away. Go to the Help menu and select Show Balloons, then move your mouse to the menu item or preference in question. To turn off Balloon Help, return to the Help menu and select Hide Balloons (see **Figure G.2**).

BBEdit Guide

BBEdit Guide (see **Figure G.3**) is a more extensive electronic help program that utilizes the Macintosh AppleGuide format. Help is available by Topics, by Index, and by keyword searching. Several tasks are explained in a step-by-step process with on-screen hints.

What's New

What's New is another help program in AppleGuide format. What's New gives a complete list of changes and updates in BBEdit 4.5. Documentation accompanies each topic (see **Figure G.4**).

Local Documentation

Bare Bones Software also provides extensive BBEdit documentation as part of the standard installation process (see **Figure G.5**).

- **What's New in BBEdit 4.5**
  covers the latest features.

- **BBEdit 4.5 Release Notes**
  covers the things you need to know to install and troubleshoot BBEdit.

- **User Manual**
  in PDF (Portable Document Format). PDF documents can be read and searched online, or printed. You'll need Adobe Acrobat Reader to view the User Manual.

- **BBEdit Extension SDK**
  information about writing your own plug-ins for BBEdit.

- **Bare Bones Guide to HTML**
  an HTML tutorial by Kevin Werbach (unaffiliated with Bare Bones and BBEdit).

- **Tech Support Bulletins**
  contains information on how to get technical support from Bare Bones.

Bare Bones Web Site

The Bare Bones Web site (see **Figure G.6**) contains everything else you'll ever need to know about BBEdit.

- Support by phone and fax
- FAQs
- Software updates
- Plug-in information
- Discussion lists
- Mailing lists
- HTML resource information

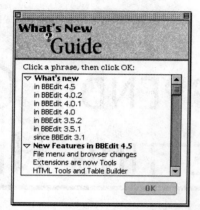

Figure G.4 The What's New guide gives you the latest scoop on BBEdit.

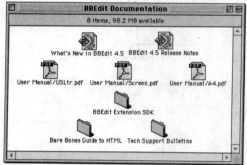

Figure G.5 BBEdit comes with plenty of detailed documentation.

Figure G.6 The official Bare Bones Web site, the final stop for your help needs.

INDEX

INDEX

# More from Peachpit Press

25 Steps to Safe Computing

Don Sellers

With planning, many computer-related health problems can be avoided. *25 Steps to Safe Computing* tells you how to reduce your risk with well-illustrated, easy-to-follow advice. It contains ergonomic tips on setting up work areas, as well as chapters on backache, headache, tendinitis, radiation, pregnancy, kid's concerns, and much more. *$5.95 (72 pages)*

America Online 3 for Macintosh: Visual QuickStart Guide

Maria Langer

–and–

America Online 3 for Windows 95: Visual QuickStart Guide

Maria Langer

With over 6 million members, America Online is the world's largest online service provider. Both Visual QuickStart Guides provide an easy, step-by-step guide for beginners to getting up and running with AOL and for intermediate users to gain more in depth understanding of the service. These books help readers go from installing the newest version of the software to exchanging e-mail, using newsgroups and the Web browser, and participating in forums and live chats. Key America Online areas, such as Entertainment, NewsStand, Computers and Software, Market-place, and Kids Only, are described and illustrated, and appendices offer lists of shortcut keys, forums, and companies. *Macintosh: $16.95 (304 pages)*
Windows 95: $17.95 (288 pages w/disk)

A Blip in the continuum, Macintosh Edition (Includes Disk)

Robin Williams and John Tollett

–and–

A Blip in the continuum, Windows Edition (Includes Disk)

Robin Williams and John Tollett

In this full-color book, author Robin Williams and illustrator John Tollett celebrate the new wave of type design known as "grunge" typography. The book consists of famous and not-so-famous quotes about type and design set in a range of grunge fonts, using rule-breaking layouts. The illustrations, created in Fractal Design Painter, complement the text. Includes a companion disk with 21 of the best freeware and shareware grunge fonts, several of which were newly created for this book. *Both versions are $22.95 (96 pages w/disk)*

CHAT

Nan McCarthy

CHAT is a fast-moving, compelling story of online romance that will appeal to all cyberjunkies and anyone looking for an entertaining story. Bev, a tough-minded book editor, cautiously begins corresponding with Maximilian, a flamboyant copywriter who approaches her after seeing her messages in an online writers forum. Their relationship gradually becomes more intense and their e-mails less inhibited as the story unfolds entirely through their messages to one another. *$7.95 (136 pages)*

Dan Gookin's Web Wambooli

Dan Gookin

Not just "another Internet book," this one showcases the perspective and experience of a computer book guru. A non-technical, jargon-limited handbook that's as entertaining as it is useful, it covers the most interesting, fun, and valuable aspects of the Internet and the World Wide Web. Covers hardware and software; choosing a service provider; using Netscape; accessing newsgroups; games, entertainment, and chat sites; and what's ahead and how to keep up. *$22.95 (400 pages)*

Director Multimedia Studio Authorized

Macromedia, Inc.

–and–

Lingo Authorized

Macromedia, Inc.

Developed by Macromedia's staff and user-tested in Macromedia's Authorized Training Centers, these large-format books include the complete curricula from the Training Centers' multi-day hands-on courses on Director 5. Master teachers present lessons in manageable step-by-step worksessions, letting you work through the courses at your own pace. The cross-platform CD-ROMs contain practice files of all lessons and demo versions of the Macromedia programs. With these Authorized books, you'll master the basics of Director in only 40 hours of hands-on training.

Director Multimedia Studio Authorized (Level 1):
$39.95 (264 pages w/CD-ROM)

Lingo Authorized (Level 2):
$39.95 (288 pages w/CD-ROM)

Elements of Web Design

Darcy DiNucci, Maria Giudice and Lynne Stiles

This book introduces graphic designers to the opportunities and pitfalls of Web design. *Elements of Web Design* includes chapters on every step of assembling pages—from practical issues, such as pulling together a team with the appropriate skills and creating contracts to reflect the ever-changing nature of Web pages, to the technical and design issues involved in creating HTML, graphics, and interactivity. Full color throughout. *$39.95 (208 pages)*

Getting Hits: The Definitive Guide to Promoting Your Website

Don Sellers

Building a world-class Web site doesn't mean people will come flocking—Web sites must be promoted to be successful. *Getting Hits* is the guidebook to the entirely new processes of advertising and publicizing that comprise promotion on the Web. Topics include posting your site to a search engine; links that give the biggest hits; guerrilla marketing strategies; producing hits offline; creating your own Web campaign; and keeping visitors coming back to your site. *$19.95 (208 pages)*

Home Sweet Home Page and the Kitchen Sink

Robin Williams with Dave Mark

This exciting new book/CD-ROM combo provides all the tools you need to get online and create Web pages. *Home Sweet Home Page and the Kitchen Sink* takes a friendly, non-technical approach to planning and designing interactive Web pages with easy-to-follow instructions and delightful illustrations. The CD-ROM provides everything else you need to finish creating your pages, including connection software for AOL, CompuServe, and AT&T. *$24.95 (208 pages)*

HTML for the World Wide Web, 2nd Edition: Visual QuickStart Guide

Elizabeth Castro

This step-by-step guide on using HTML to design pages for the World Wide Web presumes no prior knowledge of HTML, or even the Internet. It uses clear, concise instructions for creating each element of a Web page. Expanded coverage in this edition includes such major new topics as style sheets and frames, progressive JPEG images and animated GIFs, font and column width controls. *$17.95 (192 pages)*

Internet Explorer 3 for Windows 95/NT: Visual QuickStart Guide

Steven Schwartz

This book is for anyone who wants or needs to browse the World Wide Web. This hands-on guide takes a straightforward, visual approach that enables even those with little past browsing experience to get up and running quickly. New Microsoft Internet Explorer users will find the step-by-step instructions easy to follow and fun, and readers with some Microsoft Internet Explorer experience will benefit from the explanations of important new features with particular emphasis on using new plug-ins such as ActiveX and JavaScript. *$16.95 (208 pages)*

JavaScript for the World Wide Web, 2nd Edition: Visual QuickStart Guide

Tom Negrino and Dori Smith

JavaScript is a programming language designed to be used in conjunction with HTML, making HTML more powerful and interactive. All predictions are that JavaScript will become as important as HTML, and it is now fully supported in Netscape Navigator and Microsoft Internet Explorer. While other JavaScript books are intended for experienced programmers, this one is for the vast majority of HTML coders who are less technically sophisticated but still would like a useful introduction and handy reference. *$17.95 (208 pages)*

The Macintosh Bible, 6th Edition

Jeremy Judson, Editor

With over 1,000,000 copies in print, the Macintosh reference book that started it all celebrates its tenth anniversary by offering up-to-the-minute information on topics such as fonts, word processing, spreadsheets, graphics, and desktop publishing. *The Macintosh Bible, 6th Edition* tackles every subject area with a clear vision of what Macintosh users need to know in an engaging, no-nonsense style. New sections include the Internet—getting connected, sending email, surfing the Web, and downloading files; troubleshooting—revised and expanded, including details on error message codes; and Home Offices—using your Mac at home for fun and profit *$29.95 (992 pages)*

Netscape 3 for Macintosh: Visual QuickStart Guide

Elizabeth Castro

–and–

Netscape 3 for Windows: Visual QuickStart Guide

Elizabeth Castro

This book is the perfect introduction to the latest version of Netscape, the most widely used browser of the World Wide Web. You'll learn how to transfer files, read and send e-mail, use the address book, and post to newsgroups. Additionally, the book covers Netscape Gold, with helpful information on how to format your own Web page.
Macintosh: $16.95 (208 pages)
Windows: $16.95 (288 pages)

The Non-Designer's Web Book

Robin Williams and John Tollett

In the best-selling *The Non-Designer's Design Book*, Robin Williams explained design principles and techniques to novices. Now Robin does it again, but this time for the Web. This book explores basic, universal Web design principles. Using full-color examples, the book demonstrates why Web design is different from print design, how to use typography on the Web, where to get graphics, and how to get your well-designed Web site up for all to admire. *$29.95 (288 pages)*

The PC Bible, Second Edition

Eric Knorr

The PC universe is expanding, and the second edition of *The PC Bible* has grown along with it. Sixteen industry experts collaborated on this definitive guide to PCs, now updated to include Windows 95 and Internet access. Beginning and advanced users will benefit from this book's clear, entertaining coverage of fonts, word processing, spreadsheets, graphics, desktop publishing, databases, communications, utilities, multimedia, games, and more. Winner of a 1994 Computer Press Award. *$29.95 (1000 pages)*

PageMill 2 for Macintosh: Visual QuickStart Guide

Maria Langer

–and–

PageMill 2 for Windows: Visual QuickStart Guide

Maria Langer

These Visual QuickStart Guides are richly illustrated, step-by-step guides to using all the features of PageMill. As with all books in Peachpit's highly successful Visual QuickStart series (with more than a million copies in print), information is presented in a graphic, visual fashion, with hundreds of screenshots accompanied by clear instructions and loads of helpful tips.
Both versions are $15.95 (184 pages)

Real World QuarkImmedia

David Blatner

QuarkImmedia is a new product which enables designers to create interactive presentations while working in the familiar XPress environment. *Real World QuarkImmedia* covers making the transition from press to multimedia, building an infrastructure, buttons and menus, animations, sound, QuickTime, building scripts, and exporting projects (including how to export to the Web). The accompanying CD-ROM includes sample Immedia projects, the entire book in Immedia format, and many of the essential ingredients people need to create their own multimedia projects, including buttons, background art, sounds, animations, clip art, and software to help in publishing for the Internet and on CD-ROMs.
$39.95 (464 pages w/CD-ROM)

The Painter 4 Wow! Book

Cher Threinen-Pendarvis

Fractal Design Painter has so many features even power users don't know all the tricks. Whatever your skill level, you'll scurry to the computer to try out the examples in *The Painter 4 Wow! Book*. This full-color volume uses hundreds of stunning, original illustrations depicting Painter's full range of styles and effects. Step-by-step descriptions clearly explain how each piece was created by well-known artists, designers, and multimedia producers.
$44.95 (264 pages w/CD-ROM)

Shocking the Web, Macintosh Edition

Cathy Clarke, Lee Swearingen, and David K. Anderson

–and–

Shocking the Web, Windows Edition

Cathy Clarke, Lee Swearingen, and David K. Anderson

Shocking the Web is an authoritative hands-on guide by the creators of Macromedia's original Shockwave Web site that shows Director developers how to create high impact, low-bandwidth movies for the Internet. *Shocking the Web* uses detailed case studies and step-by-step design examples throughout to guide developers in creating multimedia content within the Internet's bandwidth limitations. The authors reveal Lingo tips, tricks, and secrets and cover integration of Shockwave with Java. The CD-ROM includes the case studies and design examples, as well as tutorials, template files, setup software, a save-disabled version of Director, and Shockwave clip media for Internet development.
Both versions are $44.95 (464 pages)

Web Graphics Tools and Techniques

Peter Kentie

This book is an indispensable resource for Web site creators needing to master a variety of authoring and graphics tools. It begins with basic Web concepts, then proceeds into the specifics of formatting graphics, text, and tables with HTML. Next, it moves deeper into graphics techniques, explaining the use of such tools as Photoshop, Painter, Poser, KPT Welder, GIF Construction Set, and Director. Also covers advanced issues such as tables, clickable maps, 3-D images, and user interaction. Full color throughout.
$39.95 (320 pages)

What's on the Internet, 3rd Edition

Eric Gagnon

This new edition is bigger and better than ever, with entirely updated reviews and a greatly expanded business section. *What's on the Internet* provides an informative, fun, and useful way to find out what online discussion and information groups exist on the Internet and how to connect with them. There are mini-reviews of 2,300 of the most popular newsgroups, a bonanza of Frequently Asked Question (FAQ) files, a 5,500-word subject index, and a list of more than 8,000 Internet newsgroups. *$19.95 (440 pages)*

Order Form

USA 800-283-9444 • 510-524-2178 • fax 510-524-2221
Canada 800-387-8028 • 416-447-1779 • fax 800-456-0536 or 416-443-0948

Qty	Title	Mac or Win	Price	Total

*We are required to pay sales tax in all states with the exceptions of AK, DE, MT, NH, OR, and WY. Please include appropriate sales tax if you live in any state not mentioned above.

Shipping is by UPS ground: $4 for first item, $1 each add'l.

Subtotal	
Add Applicable Sales Tax*	
Shipping	
TOTAL	

PEACHPIT PRESS 1249 EIGHTH ST. • BERKELEY, CA 94710 • WWW.PEACHPIT.COM

CUSTOMER INFORMATION

Name

Company

Street Address

City   State   Zip

Phone (   )   Fax (   )
[required for credit card orders]

PAYMENT METHOD

❏ Check enclosed   ❏ VISA   ❏ MasterCard   ❏ AMEX

Credit Card #   Exp. date

TELL US WHAT YOU THINK

Please tell us what you thought of this book.
Title:

What other books would you like us to publish?

MAC